T[...] to

Books for
Teenagers

Rough Guides online

www.roughguides.com

Rough Guide Credits

Text editors: Joe Staines, Andrew Dickson
Series editor: Mark Ellingham
Production: Julia Bovis
Layout: Katie Pringle
Proofreading: Carole Mansur

Publishing Information

This edition published November 2003 by Rough Guides Ltd,
80 Strand, London WC2R 0RL

Distributed by the Penguin Group

Penguin Books Ltd, 80 Strand, London WC2R 0RL
Penguin Putnam, Inc., 375 Hudson Street, New York 10014, USA
Penguin Books Australia Ltd, 487 Maroondah Highway,
PO Box 257, Ringwood, Victoria 3134, Australia
Penguin Books Canada Ltd, 10 Alcorn Avenue, Toronto,
Ontario, Canada M4V 1E4
Penguin Books (NZ) Ltd, 182–190 Wairau Road, Auckland 10, New Zealand

Typeset to an original design by Henry Iles

Printed in Spain by GraphyCems

© Nicholas Tucker and Julia Eccleshare, 2002
320pp, includes index
A catalogue record for this book is available from the British Library.
ISBN 1-84353-138-0

The Rough Guide to

Books for Teenagers

by
Nicholas Tucker and Julia Eccleshare

Contents

Introduction

The *Rough Guide to Books for Teenagers* recommends over 200 entertaining, moving, exciting, and challenging books. As in the two previous Rough Guides to Children's Books, our aim has been to include the best of the most popular and the most popular of the best. Titles have been grouped into eleven different categories, which broadly correspond to different genres, beginning with *Love, Sex and Change* and ending with *Humour*. While the majority of the books selected are fiction, there is also a short non-fiction section, entitled *Real Lives*, that consists of memoirs, autobiography, and travel books. Each book has a short review, with an outline of the plot followed by the reasons why we think it's worth reading. The occasional quotation helps to give a taste of what's to come, and we often suggest other works by the same author that are equally good. Because several of the titles are quite disturbing in their subject matter, each book comes with a suggested age recommendation.

We hope that *Rough Guide to Books for Teenagers* provides something for everyone, and will point readers towards books that will stay with them for the rest of their lives. Many writers have a way of putting things that makes more immediate sense than anything picked up from day-to-day conversations or entertainment, and we are confident that the selected titles will be as readable and involving for you as they are for us. Not every book will work with every reader, but we're sure that many of these books will give you that buzz of excitement and recognition that the best literature has always provided. Enjoy the feast!

acknowledgements

As always. our many friends in the world of children's publishing have provided unfailingly positive help. Working with such a friendly as well as efficient group of people has been a pleasure in itself. At Rough Guides we would like to thank Mark Ellingham, who first had the idea for these guides, and Joe Staines, whose efficient but always amiable editing skills has made writing these guides so much easier. Thanks too should go to Andrew Dickson for his contribution throughout the series and to Katie Pringle for typesetting this particular volume.

This book is dedicated with love to Henry, George, Vanessa and Edward Hammond (JE) and to Archie Holdway and Lydia Tucker (NT) – teenage readers past, present and future.

---

love, sex and change

Alain-Fournier
Le Grand Meaulnes
Penguin

Everything changes for François, the 15-year-old narrator of this story, on the day that Augustin Meaulnes comes to stay as a lodger. Two years older than François, Augustin is soon established as a natural leader at the local school. Yet one day he unaccountably disappears, riding out in a farmer's cart to an unknown destination. Four days later he returns, but as if under a spell. In strict confidence, he tells François of his accidental discovery of a strange, dream-like place where he attends a lavish and graceful fête. There he also meets Yvonne de Galais, a beautiful girl of his own age with whom he immediately falls in love. All Augustin can think about is returning to this mysterious place in order to meet her once more. But

Alain-Fournier Le Grand Meaulnes

when he tries again he can no longer find the way. Some time later Augustin does meet and marry Yvonne. But perhaps this great happiness was too much for him to believe in after so many years of searching, and his story ends sadly.

The author was only 26 years old when this story was written. Two years later he was one of the many to die

love, sex and change

during World War I, leaving just this one novel behind. It was based on the real-life courtship of his own young wife, and few other stories have ever captured the particular, bittersweet nature of first love when it is thwarted for so long, as happens here. Such strong love at a young age has the power to transform everyday reality into something magical, which is exactly what happens to Augustin when he wanders into the lost domain where he first meets Yvonne. But what seemed like a dream turns into a reality that never quite lives up to its earlier, fantastic promise. One of the great love stories of all time, this fine novel, expertly translated by Frank Davison, is quite unforgettable.

Recommended age: 15+

David Almond
Counting Stars
Hodder

The best short stories can say as much – and be as memorable – as any novel, and such is the case with this collection of eighteen stories describing the experience of growing up in a large family in the northeast of England. Brothers and sisters, aunts, grandparents and cousins come and go, observed and sometimes wondered at by the boy narrator. There is a strange visit to a fun fair, a meeting with some ragged gypsy children, a first kiss, and struggles with the strict Roman Catholic faith both at home and school. The stories are a reminder of how even the most ordinary of

everyday events can sometimes seem extraordinary. On the face of it nothing much happens, but although the thoughts, feelings and situations are not unusual, they're conveyed with all the freshness of someone experiencing them for the first time.

The author of bestselling novels such as *Skellig* and *Kit's Wilderness*, David Almond proves with *Counting Stars* to be just as at home writing small pieces. Using a minimal number of words, and avoiding lengthy build-ups or explanations, he allows the reader to work out what is really happening – often before the narrator fully understands events himself.

Recommended age: 15+

Jane Austen
Emma
Penguin

Emma Woodhouse, 'handsome, clever, and rich, with a comfortable home and happy disposition', is not quite 21 when the novel opens. Set in the early part of the nineteenth century, when the author's own brother was fighting in the Napoleonic Wars, Emma's story centres largely on the small English town where she lives, the friends she has, and the trouble she causes by meddling in their affairs. Emma thinks she is in love with someone already spoken for, and then worries that she has lost the man – Mr Knightly – that she really wanted all along. Everything finally comes together by the end, with Emma not just older but also more thoughtful after various adventures of the heart.

> 66 **The real evils indeed of Emma's situation were the power of having rather too much her own way, and disposition to think a little too well of herself; these were the disadvantages which threatened alloy to her many enjoyments. 99**

Jane Austen's concern that no one but her would much like her heroine has proved unfounded. Emma is sometimes vain, self-satisfied and insensitive, but this makes her all the more human. She is also high-spirited, affectionate and determined to make the most of her life. The author describes this young woman and those surrounding her with a quiet amusement that never turns into moral scolding. Main characters soon reveal themselves for what they are, with chief offenders including Miss Bates, the village bore; Mr

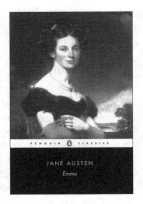

Elton, the conceited clergyman with a ghastly, snobbish wife; and Emma's own self-pitying and spoilt father. Many other minor characters fill the stage in a story that is wise as well as witty, written by one of the greatest of all English novelists.

Recommended age: 13+

Judy Blume
Forever
Macmillan

Katherine, aged 17, meets Michael at a party. He is the same age and, like her, a well-off American living in New Jersey. The two of them like each other immediately, go out for several dates and then, after some hesitation since Katherine is still a virgin, make love. This is something Katherine finds she can't discuss with her parents, but her grandmother soon finds out and advises a speedy visit to the local family planning clinic. But her parents suspect something, and send her off to summer camp in the hope she will meet other young people. She does, most particularly 21-year-old tennis coach Theo. As their romance grows, the memory of Michael is gradually shoved aside, despite the daily letters he keeps sending, all finishing with the word 'forever'.

As the first teenage story to describe sexual activity in any reasonable detail, this novel, first published in 1976, was banned in certain parts of America. Judy Blume had already written frankly for teenagers, but *Forever* went much further. This was partly in response to the thousands of letters she received from teenagers

love, sex and change

complaining that adults told them nothing about sexual matters. While sex education lessons at school have, to an extent, taken over this task, *Forever* is still an involving and persuasive story about the confused feelings common during the teenage years, and the way that sex itself can both simplify and complicate relationships.

Recommended age: 13+

Charlotte Brontë
Jane Eyre
Penguin

Jane is a plain, 10-year-old orphan, living with a mean aunt and her selfish, bullying children. When she finally rebels against her ill treatment, Jane is sent away to an equally awful boarding school. But she survives, making friends and eventually getting a job as governess to the daughter of the moody and mysterious Mr Rochester of Thornfield Hall. Despite the attentions of other beautiful women, Mr Rochester falls in love with Jane. Tragically their wedding ceremony is dramatically interrupted, when a dark secret from Mr Rochester's past catches up with him. Jane runs off into the night; years later, after many more adventures, she meets Mr Rochester once again, with happier results.

love, sex and change

I have told you, reader, that I had learnt to love Mr Rochester: I could not unlove him now, merely because I found that he had ceased to notice me...

Although it was written in 1847, much of this superb story reads as freshly today as when it was first published. As a child, Jane is outspoken, affectionate and no respecter of authority, especially when it is unjust. She is also witty and self-possessed as an adult, well able to hold her own with those richer than herself. Her love affair with Mr Rochester is always passionate, and includes a magical moment when she hears his voice calling out to her from afar just as she is about to make an unwise marriage to her clergyman cousin, the nice but stuffy St John Rivers. The description of the time spent with his intensely religious family lacks the electrifying quality of the earlier parts of this novel, but it is well worth hanging on for one of the most moving endings of any story ever written.

Recommended age: 15+

love, sex and change

Kate Cann

Diving In

Scholastic

Colette hears a lot about men from her mother's female friends. Divorced, separated or whatever, they have plenty of negative views about relationships and their pitfalls – and most of all about the awfulness of men. But Coll is 17 and she likes boys and, along with the rest of her friends, wants one of her own. Opportunities are scarce as she's at an all-girl's school, thanks to her mother's views on girls and work, but there is Art, whom she meets at swimming. Art seems to be everything that Coll has imagined, and suddenly she's changed.

Coll tells her story with a pleasing naivety, charting the important details as she and Art move from being merely swimming friends to the first overheated steps of going out together. All is told with immediacy and honesty: how Coll copes with his family, how her friends see her now and, above all, how she adjusts her self-image and learns to cope with her new feelings.

The success of *Diving In* lies in its absolute reality: Kate Cann covers the flood of emotions that threaten to overtake Coll in her first serious relationship. Her feelings and concerns about how far she wants to go with a sexual relationship with Art are intelligently handled, reflecting the confusion many girls feel about their first sexual experiences. The story of Coll and Ant continues with *In the Deep End* and *Sink or Swim* – both published by Scholastic.

Recommended age: 15+

love, sex and change

Aidan Chambers
Postcards From No Man's Land
Bodley Head

From its arresting opening, as Jacob is first befriended
and then mugged by a boy whom he mistakes for a girl,
Postcards From No Man's Land is full of surprises and
unanswered questions. Initially much of the story is
ambiguous. Jacob, on his own in Holland, standing in
for his grandmother Geertrui at his grandfather's grave
in a battle cemetery ceremony, stumbles from one
incident to another. He visits Anne Frank's house (a
solemn pilgrimage, as he confides that he sometimes
feels closer to Anne than to any living person); he meets
a group of students, some gay and some not, among
whom he quickly finds his own place; and he becomes
an active participant in Geertrui's decision to take her
own life.

> 66 For the next few minutes he indulged in a
> bout of self-loathing, his mood encouraged
> by the rain. Hamlet was dead right. How
> weary, stale, flat and unprofitable were all the
> uses of this world. How sullied he was
> himself. 99

Gradually the links between these people, their
behaviour and the things that influence them emerge,
and the story's two strands – one following present-day
Jacob, the other the grandfather for whom he was
named – are brought close to one another. In both, a

love, sex and change

background of friendship and love across ages provides Jacob with the opportunity to grow, changing from hesitant observer to emancipated thinker as he considers the things that affect him directly – such as his own sexuality, the wider morality of euthanasia and the historical impact of war and the changes it effects. Aidan Chambers won the Carnegie Medal for this beautifully written and emotionally inspiring story of adolescence.

Recommended age: 15+

Sharon Creech
Chasing Redbird
Macmillan

It's easy to identify with Zinny in this warm and funny story about the confusions of growing up and the need to find a true sense of yourself. Her rumbustious family, with its three boys and four girls, lives in a rambling farm with their aunt and uncle just next door. For Zinny, Uncle Nate's and Aunt Jessie's house has always been a sanctuary where she can talk and be heard, something she finds hard in her own home. But when her beloved Aunt Jessie dies unexpectedly, Zinny finds it difficult to get her bearings. Her thoughts are like tangled spaghetti and she cannot put them back in order. In the midst of her noisy, disorganized family she becomes increasingly silent, trying to work out for herself what she is feeling and why. She's on a private journey of discovery and she finds the perfect way to pursue it when she comes across a long-forgotten trail in the woods near her home.

Stone by stone, inch by inch, Zinny attempts to uncover the path which helps her to unravel the secrets of her aunt's life, while also making sense of the family stories she's been brought up with – and especially the details of her own childhood. And always in the background is Jake Boone, whose gifts to Zinny become increasingly ridiculous as he tries to show her how much he loves her. Zinny emerges from her task with a clearer mind – and with strong feelings for Jake.

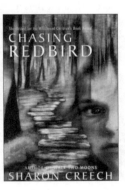

Recommended age: 11+

Charles Dickens
David Copperfield
Penguin

Young David has a poor start in life, with his father dying soon after his birth. But he and his pretty, but

13

innocent, young mother get on very well until the arrival of a new stepfather, the brutal and scheming Mr Murdstone, who is accompanied by his horrible sister Jane. David's life becomes so miserable that he runs away to stay with his eccentric aunt Betsey Trotwood. She refuses to return him, particularly as David's mother has by now died – bullied to an early

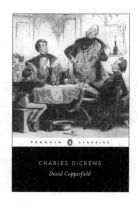

grave by her evil husband. Many more adventures follow as David survives school and then becomes a writer, finally seeing off another villain, the repulsive Uriah Heep, who is out to ruin the father of David's new love Agnes.

David Copperfield was Dickens' favourite among his own novels, and it was partly based on actual events in his own life. The hopelessly disorganized and self-deceiving Mr Micawber, with whom David lodges when he first comes to London, was inspired by the author's own father. Many other larger-than-life characters crowd these pages, all described with an energy and level of invention found in few other novelists then or since. It is a long story, written for a time when there was no competing film or television, and the first two hundred pages are particularly memorable. These describe David's boyhood at home and school, as well as the time he spent working in a factory while still a child. This was another experience shared by the author, one that was so painful to him that he could never bring himself to discuss it openly – even as an adult.

Recommended age: 13+

Berlie Doherty
Dear Nobody
Puffin

Helen and Chris have their futures mapped out: he's off to Newcastle, while she's going on to study in Manchester. But all that's a long way off in October, when school's over and they start the next part of their lives. Then, when 17-year-old Helen becomes pregnant, everything changes. Long before the pregnancy test confirms it, she can feel the changes in her body and sense the new and fragile life growing inside. It's so powerful and so private that at first Helen feels utterly alone. There's just her and the baby – Nobody. Then she must tell Chris. What will he say? They'd never talked of babies – or even a future together. And how can she tell her mother?

66 You didn't ask my permission to plant yourself in me, after all. You're like one of those sycamore trees that keep sprouting up from nowhere in our garden. Mum always tugs them out. 'We don't want you here,' she says.

I know just what she means. 99

love, sex and change

Alone and frightened, in the end Helen shares her secret with them and finds herself swept along by their reactions. Plans are made: Helen and Chris don't want a baby to stop them; they have the rest of their lives to consider. Then Helen changes her mind. However hard it is, she finds that the love between herself and the baby growing inside is the most important thing, even though it means breaking her ties with Chris in order to keep going. 'Dear Nobody', she writes to the unknown but increasingly precious child, recording her thoughts and feelings, the way she changes and the decisions she makes about her life and the baby's future. But this is Chris's story, too, and the two are told together as Chris reads Helen's letter to the baby. His feelings about Helen, about being a father and, above all, about his own mother – who left when he was child – are gradually explored.

Recommended age: 13+

Jennifer Donnelly
A Gathering Light
Bloomsbury

Life looks exceedingly grim to Mattie, the 15-year-old daughter of a widowed American farmer with a large family but slender means. While she longs for further education, her father insists that she stay at home in order to bring up the rest of the family. Starvation is never far away after a bad harvest or serious illness, and how Mattie just manages to cope will be an eye-opener for modern readers reared in more affluent times. The date is 1906, and the setting is Big Moose Lake, a summer playground for wealthy New Yorkers. But Mattie also becomes involved with the real-life tragedy of Grace Brown and her no-good lover Chester Gillette.

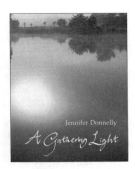

Jennifer Donnelly
A Gathering Light

Drawing on actual letters written by Grace at the time, the sad, sordid murder story from long ago is skilfully woven into the rest of this well-written book, as satisfying as a substantial, no-frills meal after a tiring day. Mattie herself may be too good to be true in her role as perfect substitute mother at home and fairy godmother to everyone else outside, but the tough reality of her daily life in the most primitive surroundings means that the story always stays believable. Even when she wins the attentions of the most handsome boy in town, the fantasy is brought down to earth when it turns out that he is also after a section of her father's untended land. When she finally escapes to a better life elsewhere, every reader will be rooting for her.

Recommended age: 13+

Roddy Doyle
Paddy Clarke Ha Ha Ha

Minerva

Mixing observations of childish innocence and adult worldliness to create a funny but acute picture of

love, sex and change

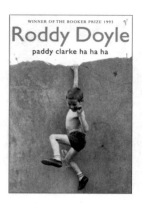

love, sex and change

growing up, Roddy Doyle draws deeply on his own childhood in *Paddy Clarke Ha Ha Ha*. The young Paddy is brought up in Barrytown, a poor suburb of Dublin. As a child, there are the certainties that make him safe. There's home with his Ma and Da, a younger brother whom he loves and scorns at the same time and the baby sisters whose endless demand for clean nappies forces the young Paddy to spend hours at the mangle; there's school with its familiar rituals and humiliations; and then there's Paddy's tight circle of friends, with whom he roams the neighbourhood, exploring the promising terrain of the building sites, scrapping and squabbling but essentially supporting each other.

But things in Paddy's world are changing. What he has taken for granted emotionally and physically is disappearing. Bewilderingly, there is violence between his parents and long silences which are hard to explain. Blaming himself, Paddy hatches plans to make things better, believing that he plays a central role and can therefore affect the outcome. Outside the house, too, the endless wasteland is being built up with new homes, and the boys' playground is gone. In all respects Paddy's world is diminishing as childhood ends. He begins to look back at it, seeing what he had taken for granted in a new light. By capturing the tiny details of one boy's life and by the use of sparkling dialogue, Roddy Doyle makes Paddy's story immediate – while also asserting some universal truths about growing up.

Recommended age: 15+

F. Scott Fitzgerald
The Great Gatsby
Penguin

All anyone knows about Jay Gatsby is that he is a young American who gives superb parties in his lavish Long Island home. But Nick, the narrator, finds out that Gatsby grew up poor before unexpectedly coming into some money, perhaps through involvement with local crooks. But however corrupt he is in real life, Gatsby remains true to his fantasy about getting together with Daisy, a girl he has always loved but who is married to someone else. His parties are now thrown in order to attract Daisy, but when they finally meet up again she rejects him once more. In the end Gatsby eventually becomes the victim of the thoughtlessness of his rich friends 'who smashed up

F. Scott Fitzgerald The Great Gatsby

love, sex and change

things and creatures and then retreated back into their money or their vast carelessness'.

> ❝ If personality is an unbroken series of successful gestures, then there was something gorgeous about him, some heightened sensitiveness to the promises of life, as if he were related to one of those machines that register earthquakes ten thousand miles away. ❞

Written in 1926, *The Great Gatsby* is one of the finest love stories. Gatsby himself is a vivid example of the American dream, in that he is determined to get what he wants without ever accepting that it might never happen. Although maintaining this illusion finally leads to tragedy, he remains something of a hero. Surrounded by crowds of hangers-on out to get their hands on as much of his wealth as they can, Gatsby is too obsessed with the beautiful Daisy to bother about what is happening in the rest of his life. Written in spare, direct prose in under two hundred pages, this compelling story stays in the memory long after it's been read.

Recommended age: 15+

E.M. Forster
A Room with a View
Penguin

Lucy Honeychurch is on holiday in Florence. It's early in the twentieth century so, as a young woman on her own, she has to be accompanied, in this case by her ghastly older cousin Charlotte. One day, after going out on her own, Lucy witnesses a quarrel that leads to a murder. Fainting on the spot, she is rescued by George Emerson, a young Englishman staying at the same hotel. Because he has an unconventional father and himself works only as a clerk on the railways, snobbish Charlotte decides he is unsuitable company for her wealthy young niece. But after a dramatic picnic and many other incidents, things work out differently, with Charlotte herself, very much against her will, finally succeeding in bringing the two young people together.

The author was always in revolt against the mean-spirited, class-conscious ways of so many middle-class Britons at the time he was writing. He also loved Italy, where he believed people lived a more natural, instinctive type of life. But rather than preach this message, he gets it across through gentle observation and quiet humour, letting his least favourite characters condemn themselves out of their own mouths. Understated and quietly amusing, Forster's novels show him to be one of the best as well as wisest of early twentieth-century writers, creating stories that are always far deeper than they seem at first sight.

Recommended age: 15+

love, sex and change

Adèle Geras
The Tower Room
Red Fox

Based on the fairy story of
Rapunzel, in which the
beautiful young girl
imprisoned in the tower lets
down her golden hair so that
her lover can climb up to her,
The Tower Room cleverly
blends the romance of a fairy
tale into the realities of a
modern love story.

Megan, Bella and Alice
have been schoolfriends since
their arrival at Egerton Hall.
Shut away within the
confines of the boarding house, they've shared
everything, preparing themselves for life outside. But
it's a fanciful kind of preparation which leaves the girls
yearning for anything that will take them over the
threshold into adulthood. Now in their final year, the
girls are allowed a room far removed from the rest of
the school and it's here, up in the 'Tower', that Megan
first sees Simon climbing up the scaffolding towards
her room. Megan falls for him instantly and slips
readily out of her old life and into a new one.

Adèle Geras's storytelling delicately charts the
overwhelming emotions of falling in love. Megan's
transformation from schoolgirl to young woman is

beautifully and convincing described, capturing the
importance of falling in love while not diminishing the
difficulties that it can bring. *The Tower Room* is the first
in a trilogy, and is followed by *Pictures of the Night* and
Watching the Roses.

Recommended age: 13+

Thomas Hardy
Tess of the D'Urbervilles
Penguin

Tess is the teenage daughter of an unsuccessful farmer
living in the West Country. After quitting home she is
seduced by her cousin Alec, who then leaves her with a
baby who dies at birth. But the disgrace of having a
child born outside marriage means that Tess feels she
has a terrible secret to hide.

When Angel Clare, a
clergyman's son, later courts
her, Tess keeps silent about
her past, telling him
everything only on their
wedding night. Angel can't
bear what he hears, and
leaves Tess – who is then
pestered by Alec once more.

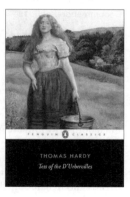

This story was considered
deeply shocking when it was
first published in 1891, and
it continues to pack a

23

powerful punch over a hundred years later. Tess seems to act like a magnet to evil or weak men, and the way things always work out for the worst seems like a tragic game played out by fate on a defenceless young girl. But Hardy always believed we should never expect fairness from what he saw as a meaningless universe ruled by chance rather than by divine mercy.

> **She had never cared for him, she did not care for him now. She had dreaded, winced before him, succumbed to him. And that was all.**

Despite this pessimistic vision, there are many beautiful moments in the book, particularly the descriptions of the traditional life of country people, that even then was beginning to disappear with the arrival of new attitudes and ways of doing things.

Recommended age: 15+

Ruth Elwin Harris
The Silent Shore
Walker

The four Purcell sisters are talented, liberated and fiercely independent. Orphaned young, Frances and Julia, both of whom are gifted painters, along with the more homely Gwen, take care of the youngest, Sarah, trying to give her the kind of life that their parents would have wanted. Advice comes from their close friends and neighbours the Mackenzies, a conventional but well-meaning couple whose sons are sometimes

SISTERS OF THE QUANTOCK HILLS

The Silent Shore

Ruth Elwin Harris

brothers and sometimes lovers to the powerful Purcell sisters.

This, the first of a quartet, is Sarah's story. It begins in 1910 at a time when it seems as if summer will never end, when life in the Quantock Hills of Somerset is a long round of idyllic outings. As the youngest, Sarah yearns to be included by the older ones on their expeditions and fiercely resists attempts to send her away to school. She treasures the moments of kindness from the glamorous Mackenzie boys and she is baffled by her sisters' frequent bantering quarrels with them, aware of currents of strong feelings but not quite aware enough to interpret them accurately.

But times are changing – and fast. The comfortable way of life of the Purcells and the Mackenzies is ended for ever by the outbreak of World War I, when Geoffrey and Gabriel Mackenzie go off to fight. Even Antony joins up, although he's under age. There are rows about socialism, the Fabians and the war itself. Then there's the waiting, and the bad news that was to become so familiar to a generation of parents. Sarah observes it all as she grows up, moving from a child to an adult and from an old social order to a new one.

Recommended age: 11+

love, sex and change

Lesley Howarth
Carwash
Puffin

Fifteen-year-old Luke, the narrator of this story, has a flourishing carwash business that he operates after school and in the holidays. His neighbour, Bix, who is the same age, has different interests, spending most of her time up a tree. There is also clumsy Danny, Luke's brother, and beautiful Liv, Bix's sister. They all spend the summer together along with a cast of minor characters,

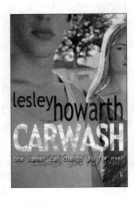

each one pursuing their own interests whenever they meet, argue, and in the case of Luke fall heavily in love. Eventually Liv has to make an enormous personal decision, Luke gets to know Danny better and Bix finally comes out of her shell. As they all discover in their different ways, just one summer can change you for ever.

66 Disaster-man guns the throttle. The wheels spin round in the mud. Now I have to dig him out of a mess, just like I do every day. Give Danny a stereo, knobs fall off it. A jar to unscrew, he'll break it. A disaster waiting to happen, that's what Danny is. 99

Some writers achieve their effects by creating high
drama peopled by outsize characters, but Lesley
Howarth is the opposite. This story is based on a village
she knew and on what happened there to one of her
best friends. Telling much of the story through
dialogue, there are no wasted words in this humane and
touching story. Everything is totally believable, as are
the various quirky, and sometimes irritating, characters.
The atmosphere of a long hot summer in which little
seems to be happening but which in fact is packed with
drama for those most closely involved is expertly
caught. Lesley Howarth is one of the very best writers
for teenagers, and this is her finest novel so far – easy to
read, never predictable, often wickedly funny and
entirely original.

Recommended age: 13+

Tove Jansson
The Summer Book
Sort Of Books

Translated by Thomas Teal, *The Summer Book* is a
delicately told collection of incidents that happen
during one long summer that Sophia spends with her
grandmother. They live on a tiny island far from
everywhere in the Gulf of Finland, in a little cabin on
the seashore. Together they explore every inch of the
island, telling each other stories, weaving fantasies
around the birds and trees, carving boats out of bark,
making their own miniature worlds and learning about

love, sex and change

the past. Grandmother is imaginative, wise and very funny; she helps Sophia to learn about every fragile plant and bird on the island. There's moss that will spring back only once after it's walked on: after that it never comes up again. And similarly there is the lapwing which can be frightened only once before it flies away for ever. Sophia's mother is dead and her grandmother helps her to overcome her loneliness and fears by sympathetic subterfuge, never by bossy instruction. And she lets Sophia be free to do as she pleases, so long as it's kindly meant. In one of the best chapters, she helps Sophia to manage the very difficult friend who comes to stay – a girl whom Sophia rather foolishly admired but who turns out to be a hopeless guest.

> **One time in April there was a full moon, and the sea was covered in ice. Sophia woke up and remembered that they had come back to the island and that she had a bed to herself because her mother was dead.**

The Summer Book is based on Tove Jansson's own island experiences and her relationship with her granddaughter Sophia and, through them, she captures the universals of a special place and the cementing of a very special relationship in it.

Recommended age: 11+

James Joyce
A Portrait of the Artist as a Young Man
Penguin

Through the character of Stephen Dedalus, James Joyce tells the story of what often seems to be his own life, from his first memories of childhood to his feelings as a young man on the point of leaving Ireland. His perceptions are precise and incredibly vivid at every age – partly because he adapts his style as he tells the story, starting with tiny domestic details such as the distinctive smells of his parents and even the smell of the oil sheet when he wets the bed.

Sent away to boarding school at the age of 6, he describes the bewilderment of school life and, above all, his intense desire to fit in – even though he always finds it hard to understand exactly what the rules are. It's a theme that recurs throughout as Stephen remains an outsider, attempting to accept the prevailing orthodoxies of his childhood, which his peers seem to understand so easily, as well as the political

love, sex and change

29

views of his father and, more intensely, the religious beliefs of his mother. He almost conforms on the religious front after his first sexual experience brings deep feelings of guilt and shame. To absolve himself, Stephen goes on a church retreat where the sermon on damnation and repentance leads him near to thinking he should become a priest. But he resists when he is reminded by seeing a beautiful woman of what he would have to give up and of why beauty matters.

Stephen's attempts at conformity are largely doomed to failure – his questioning mind and desire to be free are at least as strong as his need to fit in. *A Portrait of the Artist* is a book of hope, as Stephen finds himself and identifies what matters to him.

Recommended age: 15+

D.H. Lawrence
Sons and Lovers
Penguin

Paul Morel's heavy-drinking coal-miner father and his ex-schoolteacher mother do not get on. Instead Mrs Morel increasingly looks to her children for the affection and sensitivity she can't find in her husband. But as Paul grows up her possessive feelings become a burden to him, particularly when he starts dating girls. His first love, the quiet and intensely spiritual Miriam, is still bitterly resented by Mrs Morel. But when Paul falls for a married woman, his mother realizes her power over him is gone, and dies soon after from a painful illness. Released from his home ties, Paul sets

out to make his own way in the world.

This explosive story is based on the author's own early life in Eastwood, near Nottingham. It mixes loving descriptions of the surrounding countryside he knew so well with realistic dialogue and total honesty when it comes to describing the extreme emotions produced by this particular family situation. Paul both loves his mother and resents her; he also finds himself attracted towards and repelled by his long-suffering girlfriend Miriam. But what is never in doubt is Paul's own determination to live a full life, rejecting the cramped, dangerous work of a miner for the more fulfilling existence he is determined to find for himself. The author himself was always a rebel, frequently at odds with authority. This book, published in 1913, still comes over as an act of blazing rebellion as Paul insists on maintaining his individuality against all the odds.

Recommended age: 15+

Laurie Lee
Cider with Rosie
Penguin

Laurie Lee was born in 1914, and spent most of his childhood in a small country village with his mother

love, sex and change

and three adoring, older sisters. His father rarely visited the family, leaving his disorganized but good-natured wife to bring up the children on her own. Playing with other children, learning about the different personalities in the village, watching country life going on in its traditional ways and finally attending the local school, the young Laurie has a happy childhood recalled here with a real sense of delight. His story finishes when he finally reaches adolescence and starts to write the poetry for which he later became famous, along with this autobiographical book that has long been especially popular.

> **66** I was lost and I did not expect to be found again. I put back my head and howled, and the sun hit me smartly on the face, like a bully. **99**

But despite the loving descriptions of the beauty surrounding him, from nature itself to his three, much loved sisters, this is no sentimental view of country life. The family is extremely poor, with Laurie's mother finally unable to cope when her children leave home and she is left alone. The young men of the village are also honestly portrayed, at one point brutally attacking a stranger who unwisely boasts of his wealth. Laurie and the local boys occasionally play harsh games on the domestic animals surrounding them; at other times they take it out on the various children the villagers treat as outcasts. But however bleak the long winters, the ultimate mood of this marvellous book is a celebration of life in all its aspects. This is particularly

love, sex and change

so at the moment when the young Laurie first falls for bold, pretty Rosie 'with her cat-like eyes and curling mouth'.

Recommended age: 11+

Ted van Lieshout
Brothers
Collins

Are you still a brother if your brother dies? So speculates Luke after the unexpected death of his younger brother Maus. It's just one of the questions that Luke poses for his dead sibling as he tries to work through his complicated feelings about himself as a brother and as an individual, and while he tries to let go of his brother's memory without forgetting or changing him too much.

When the boys' mother plans a bonfire to burn all of Maus's belongings, a spectacular gesture designed to rid her of his haunting presence, Luke finds he's frightened of losing him. Trying to make sense of his feelings – which include guilt at being the survivor and jealousy that his parents might not be so upset if it had been him instead – Luke writes his own entries in an old diary he once gave to his brother. Maus's brief and straightforward notes provide a point of contact for Luke as

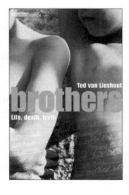

Ted van Lieshout

brothers

Life, death, truth

he charts his feelings since Maus's death. What Luke reveals has many of the universals of grief: that his parents are shut off into separate units, locked into their own feelings which are too painful and too private to share; that mourning takes a different pace for everyone and that it leaves many unanswered questions. But Luke also reveals important things particular to him and his brother.

Ted van Lieshout doesn't shy away from the most difficult of emotions. Grief doesn't pass, but it does fade away and the power of love between brothers and between parents and children remains – all forcefully conveyed in this idiomatic translation by Lance Salway.

Recommended age: 15+

Carson McCullers
The Member of the Wedding
Penguin

In the long, sultry days of summer, 12-year-old Frankie dreams of something new – something that can change her life, something that will make her belong. She is bored by the childish neighbourhood games that her friends still play, just as she's grown out of the endless games of bridge dealt out on the kitchen table with her young cousin John Henry and Berenice, the elderly housekeeper. She longs to belong to something else: something adult.

The chance to change comes with her brother's wedding. Frankie knows little about her brother or his fiancée, but she weaves a new fantasy life for herself, sure that they will be willing to take her with them into a glorious adult future. To make sure that she's properly prepared for the wedding, Frankie gives herself a new personality and sets off into town. Now called 'F. Jasmine' in an attempt to seem more feminine, she buys adult clothes and visits a bar – with near-catastrophic results. And then it's the wedding itself.

Frankie's dreams are shattered but she returns home as Frances, a new person, one who is ready to grow up.

> ❝ It happened that green and crazy summer when Frankie was twelve years old. This was the summer when for a long time she had not been a member. She belonged to no club and was a member of nothing in the world. Frankie had become an unjoined person who hung around in doorways, and she was afraid. ❞

Set over only one weekend and told in three sections in which Frankie changes from F. Jasmine to Frances, *The Member of the Wedding* is hauntingly intense in capturing the prison-like feelings of childhood and her desperate yearning to escape them.

Recommended age: 15+

love, sex and change

Ian McEwan

Atonement

Vintage

During the long hot summer of 1935, 13-year-old Briony is attempting to put on a play with her cousins, the precocious but unbiddable Lola and her unruly younger brothers. Frustrated when it goes wrong, she wanders the country-house home of her childhood. While her mother retires to her bed with a migraine, and her much-worshipped brother Leon takes his friend to sit and drink by the pool, Briony chances to see the moment when her older sister Cecilia strips off and dives into the fountain – watched, too, by Robbie, a friend of Cecilia's from Cambridge who is also the son of a family servant. Much later in the day, when Lola is assaulted in the grounds, Briony, inspired by jealousy, creates a fiction invented from what she has seen which

she cannot retract and which is to haunt her for the rest of her life.

In the two subsequent parts of the novel, the effects of Briony's story on herself, Cecilia and Robbie are exposed. Five years on, Robbie, now living with Cecilia, has been in the British evacuation from Dunkirk. His experiences as a soldier in this chaotic and destructive episode of World War II are described in sharp detail, bringing into focus the mixed emotions of war. Back in England, Cecilia and Briony work as nurses: both are changed and Briony tries to make amends, but it is far too late. In part three, Briony, resplendent on her 77th birthday, looks back on her life as a writer and what she did as a child.

Briony's story, set against a convincing background of English history over more than half a century, is compulsively readable, while also provoking thought about how partial a child's view may be – and how what happens in childhood affects adult life.

Recommended age: 15+

Michelle Magorian
A Little Love Song
Mammoth

It's wartime England and everything is slightly out of kilter. Seventeen-year-old Rose and her older sister Diana have been sent out of London after their father's death in the war. Different though the girls are from each other – Diana's the conformist, Rose the bookish rebel – both long for a summer by the sea. When they boldly take the decision to look after themselves, they know it will be a summer they'll never forget.

In their different ways, Diana and Rose explore their new freedom and break through some of the prewar restrictions. Some seem gloriously simple. Rose learns to swim and discovers a copy of *Jane Eyre*, which is on the banned list at her small-minded boarding school.

Diana learns to cook and befriends an unmarried mother, realizing that the old prejudices against women who get pregnant outside marriage make no sense in such uncertain times. But more importantly for both, they fall in love. Diana finds happiness after detaching herself from the dreary Timothy (who writes her depressing letters), while Rose uncovers a love affair from the previous war which makes a romantic background to her own gradual, unexpected but captivating romance.

Michelle Magorian writes with tremendous immediacy, so that Diana and Rose and the small community they are living in convince absolutely. *A Little Love Song* is a gloriously romantic story which also gives a vivid picture of two girls throwing over the stuffy traces of prewar England.

Recommended age: 13+

Daphne du Maurier
Rebecca
Virago

Romantic, sinister, thrilling and haunting in turns, *Rebecca* is full of suppressed passion and riddled with ambiguities. Told by the second Mrs de Winter, who remains nameless throughout, it unravels a mystery that leaves much to interpretation. After a whirlwind romance in Monte Carlo, the narrator marries Maxim de Winter and is swept off to Manderley, his beautiful home in the country. Deeply in love with Maxim, she is desperate to make him happy while always conscious that she'll never be able to replace his first wife, Rebecca, whose tragic death has caused him so much pain. She is young and inexperienced, awed by her husband's greater worldliness but shut out from what he has experienced in the past. The new Mrs de Winter tries her hardest but Manderley holds dark secrets. Something tragic and sinister lies behind the beauty and splendour, something that relates to her predecessor Rebecca – but the new Mrs de Winter cannot discover it.

Tricked by the formidable housekeeper Mrs Danvers, whose love for Rebecca makes her an implacable enemy, the new Mrs de Winter makes one hideous mistake after another. Mrs Danvers does all she can to sabotage the new marriage and all but succeeds, until the truth is at last revealed. The second Mrs de Winter's innocent misreading of Maxim's

grief and the simplicity of her love for him, contrasted with that of the sophisticated Rebecca, makes this a dark but uttely compelling love story.

Recommended age: 15+

Tony Parsons
Man and Boy
HarperCollins

Fast approaching his thirtieth birthday, Harry appears to have everything he needs: a loving wife, an adorable son and a job in television that is moving into the stratosphere of success. But in an injudicious moment he throws the whole thing away. Suddenly his wife has left him and he's lost his job. It seems like the end of everything as all the trappings of being an adult slip away. All but one. Harry retains the most important sense of purpose in his life – his son. How he manages

to cope is beautifully narrated from Harry's point of view. Standing in the middle of three generations, he reflects on the role of a father, what it means to be one and how being a successful father can best be achieved.

Man and Boy is funny and sharp about life and relationships today: Tony Parsons doesn't shy away from the complexities of family break-up, nor does he romanticize them. The life-long responsibilities are never underestimated, but the underlying joy which the father-son relationship brings shines through them all.

Recommended age: 15+

Mirjam Pressler
Shylock's Daughter
Macmillan

Both beautiful and deadly, the background of sixteenth-century Venice is richly evoked in this powerful and timeless story of love, one which cuts across cultural barriers but which cannot break them down.

Sixteen-year-old Jessica is in love – dangerous enough as it is, but her love comes at an exceptional price. The daughter of Shylock, Jessica lives in the Venetian Ghetto with all the other Jews. It's a place of safety, but also a place of imprisonment; here the Jews mix with their own kind and have their own laws and customs. Lorenzo, on the other hand, is a Christian and a nobleman. The two should never meet, especially given the hostility between their cultures. But Jessica is determined. She's tired of the rules of the Ghetto: she longs to be free and to live in the comfortable world of Lorenzo and his friends. Jessica makes her choice too lightly, little knowing that such freedom comes at a tremendous price. Even after marriage, she will always be an outsider – to both her old and her new life.

Taken from the story of Shakespeare's *Merchant of Venice*, *Shylock's Daughter* portrays life in the Venetian

love, sex and change

Ghetto vividly while also telling a story of family discord and teenage revolt. It gives powerful insights into the prejudices of the time, prejudices that are not so very different from the racial and cultural tensions of today.

Recommended age: 11+

J.D. Salinger
The Catcher in the Rye
Penguin

Expelled from his fourth private school in Pennsylvania after failing his exams, 16-year-old Holden Caulfield sets off with what money he has left to New York City. After some depressing adventures he meets a former girlfriend, and suggests they run away together. When she refuses, Holden returns home to see his much young sister Phoebe – the only person with whom he now feels at ease. Still determined to get away somewhere, he finally decides he can't leave her and stays. But this brings on the nervous breakdown that has been threatening him all the time. It then turns out that this whole book has been written by him on the advice of his psychiatrist as an attempt to work out how he has reached such a low point.

> **I'd have this rule that nobody could do anything phoney when they visited me. If anyone tried anything phoney, they couldn't stay.**

Holden himself is a pain – self-obsessed, lying and constantly showing off. But he is also extremely funny; mercilessly criticising everyone he knows – even those he has just met – in a monologue so convincing it is as if he is talking in the same room. His chief loathing is for anything he considers 'phoney' – a word freely applied to his parents, teachers, fellow pupils and almost everyone else except his little sister. Holden believes that she's too young to pretend in the way he thinks everyone else does, and he wonders whether he can save her from becoming false and insincere too. But while Holden is good at spotting the flaws in others, he can't see how immature he is himself. This novel opened the way to many other stories written as if by a young person thinking aloud, revealing their various strengths and weaknesses in the process.

Recommended age: 15+

Dodie Smith
I Capture the Castle
Virago

A charming beginning sets the scene for this unashamedly romantic, yet wonderfully observed, story of a bohemian family and their unusual life in an unusual home built within a ruined castle. It is told by 17-year-old Cassandra, who writes by candlelight in an old notebook with the stub of a pencil and tells of the Mortmains, whose life is dominated by their increasing poverty. Cassandra regards their situation as romantic,

love, sex and change

NOW A MAJOR MOTION PICTURE

STARRING MARC BLUCAS, ROSE BYRNE, SINEAD CUSACK,
TARA FITZGERALD, ROMOLA GARAI, BILL NIGHY and HENRY THOMAS

'This film has one of the most charismatic narrators I've ever met'
J. K. Rowling

I CAPTURE
THE CASTLE

DODIE
SMITH

in contrast with her sister Rose, who longs only to get out of it. The family spends much time thinking of money-making opportunities – even embroiling the visiting librarian in their bewildering discussions. There seem few ways out: there is no income and the best furniture has already been sold. Cassandra's father is a successful author, now stalled by writer's block – or, as his daughters think, insidious laziness. Their young, beautiful, lute-playing stepmother once worked as an artists' model, a job to which she's disinclined to return, while Cassandra and Rose see no way of making money except – of course – through a glorious marriage.

> **66** I write this sitting in the kitchen sink. That is, my feet are in it; the rest of me is on the draining-board, which I have padded with our dog's blanket and the tea-cosy. **99**

When the new American heirs to the neighbouring Scoatney Hall turn up, this once-remote possibility suddenly becomes a reality. As Rose is engaged to Simon, Cassandra charts the shift in the family's way of life, recognizing that wealth and happiness are not

always related, before the real romance of the story
unfolds and true happiness is found.

Recommended age: 13+

Zadie Smith
White Teeth
Penguin

White Teeth is a huge book in all respects, with multiple
plots that weave tightly into each other as the stories of
two families unravel across three generations. Told
from many different angles, it is pertinent, questioning
and illuminating and, above all, very funny about
contemporary life and the role the past has to play in it.
And it's gloriously well observed, accurately charting
changing tastes and fashions – especially about race and
class against the realistic background of Willesden and
Cricklewood in northwest
London.

Set in the last quarter of
the twentieth century as
multicultural society
properly takes root, the
families of Archibald Jones
and Samed Iqbal, two
friends whose paths first
crossed during World War
II, lurch haphazardly
through life. Saved from
attempting to commit
suicide, Archie falls into the

love, sex and change

path of the much younger Clara, herself escaping from the over-zealous religion of her mother. Samed Iqbal has aspirations to culture which he longs to bestow on his twin sons, but in his daily life he's forced to suffer the indignity of being a lowly waiter in his cousin's restaurant. From these beginnings, aspiration and reality diverge as the two marriages stagger on while their children take their own vital steps into the future.

Zadie Smith constantly moves the angles of this story, telling it from many different points of view – especially well when seen by her huge cast of adolescent characters. Real events such as the freak hurricane of 1987 are perfectly integrated into her fiction, making the imaginary plot securely based and totally convincing. Smith misses nothing in her telling of everyday life: she notes the details of food, clothes, cars and songs, and captures precisely the speech of different groups. She also builds up huge scenes effortlessly, giving *White Teeth* great energy and theatricality.

Recommended age: 15+

Sue Townsend
The Secret Diary of Adrian Mole aged 13 ³/₄
Mandarin

Adrian's take on life, as exposed in the diary which he kindly lets us read, is cheeringly optimistic – despite his uncanny capacity to find that everything goes wrong around him. He has a natural comic's ability to be laughed with as well as at: his mistakes are so endearingly convincing and, after a while, predictable.

His secret (or not so secret) longing for the largely unavailable Pandora, his spots, his parents' marriage – all of these are recorded in Adrian's diary, sometimes in tones of outrage when everything is against him, sometimes with the naive enthusiasm of a child who is, as yet, unbowed by the anxieties of adolescence. Not that Adrian doesn't worry.

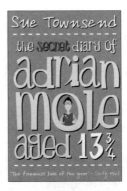

He's anxious, all right, and not surprisingly given the course his life takes and how little control he seems to have, but he's remarkably resilient and rarely complains for long. He is also growing up, so there are satisfying – if stuttering – developments in his personality.

Adrian's diary entertainingly captures the intense mood swings of adolescence, showing how fickle they can be without belittling their importance. Both for its authenticity and for its kind view of teenagers, Adrian's secret diary is reassuring reading.

Recommended age: 11+

Robert Westall
Falling into Glory
Mammoth

Robbie's adolescence is, of course, particular to him but it also captures many of of the emotions which are

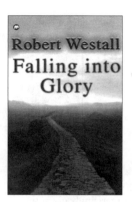

Robert Westall
Falling into Glory

universal to that period of life. He tells his story looking back from an older and more worldly perspective, recording and describing the powerful emotions which swept him along, and adding some insights which he might not have had at the time. Set at a time of grammar schools and scholarships, when knowledge of sex was limited to what little could be seen in *Picture Post*, Robbie embarks on a forbidden love affair that threatens his whole future. He is both the cleverest boy in his year and an outstanding rugby player, much admired by his peers. But where match results were once what mattered most to Robbie, suddenly they count for nothing compared with the new feelings which take him over.

Robbie has fallen in love with a teacher. Much younger than most of the rest of the staff, Miss Harris is brilliant and she encourages Robbie to be as ambitious as possible; she even offers to coach him in Latin. Robbie knows that he's falling in love, but what does Miss Harris want out of it? Interspersed with social commentary – delivered against a background of what the rugby team is up to – this is a convincing and tender love story which begins with charming, old-fashioned innocence and ends just before catastrophe strikes.

Recommended age: 13+

48

Antonia White
Frost in May
Virago

Nanda Green is only 9 years
old when she starts at the
Convent of the Five
Wounds, an austere Roman
Catholic all-girls boarding
school. Quick-witted and
willing to please, she soon
settles into a routine that
begins with a cold bath
every morning and is
governed by strict
discipline. Nanda's mother
is dismayed, on her first
visit, to hear about the
many rules and regulations,

not to mention by the sight of her small daughter
wearing compulsory grey gloves and with her hair cut
short. But Nanda initially thrives in this atmosphere,
making friends with fellow pupils and eventually
becoming deeply attached to a young nun who is also
her teacher. Then disaster strikes when, at the age of
13, the secret novel Nanda has been writing is
discovered by one of her teachers. Her harmless
romantic fantasies are condemned as filth and
impurity, and Nanda is expelled from the school she
has finally learned to love.

love, sex and change

This passionate story, written in 1933, is closely based on Antonia White's own experiences at school. Although the author remained a Roman Catholic, the novel always sides with Nanda and her attempt to preserve her own individuality. While Nanda's father remains unforgiving, her teachers recognize that although there is nothing very terrible in what she has done she is still too independent for the convent's strict, almost dictatorial regime. Nanda enjoys much of boarding school, yet there is always a part of her that questions what she is told, and it is this determination to remain true to herself that makes this such an inspiring as well as a deeply moving story.

Recommended age: 15+

Jeanne Willis
The Hard Man of the Swings
Faber

Nothing is easy for Mick. His mother has a succession of boyfriends and finally leaves home for ever, which means that Mick no longer sees his younger brother Terry, whom he adores. On top of this, things are tough at school. When Mick's weak father finally makes an appearance, it looks as if things might improve but, sickeningly, he

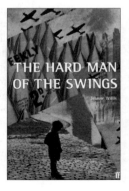

love, sex and change

turns out to be a child abuser, and Mick reacts with murderous rage when he finally realizes the truth.

> **I hold my baby sister to my chest, slam the door shut and run out into the snow. I can hear the bullets flying, I can hear my dad screaming, and it feels so good.**

Set in Britain in the 1950s, a fairly cheerless place still recovering from World War II, this novel is based upon true events. In the preface of the book is an address for readers who may have found themselves facing the same kind of dangers as Mick and who are looking for help. But although it's a bleak story, Mick's own strength and sense of hope still keep bursting through. The result is an odd mixture of sadness and humour, as Mick sizes up all the odd people he meets in his turbulent life, including a mad cousin who lusts after him at every opportunity. Well written in dialogue that is always realistic if seldom polite, the book ends just as Mick is facing one of his worst crises. Yet, whatever the odds, there's a feeling that he will somehow survive, with the help of the few supportive characters among all the others who let him down.

Recommended age: 13+

Jacqueline Wilson
Girls in Love
Corgi

Year Nine: a time of intense friendships (and rivalries) and, above all, a time for falling in love. Ellie narrates this

love, sex and change

chatty story of her gang – best friends Nadine and Magda – and their various fantasy boyfriends, real boyfriends and friends who are boys. But it's all so difficult when the moment of change comes. Now it's Nadine and Liam, Magda and Greg – and Ellie and no one. Ellie's anguish when the other two pair off is tangible: they can discuss kissing, for instance, and she's got nothing to say. So Ellie takes a drastic step to survive: she invents a boyfriend. Luckily there's Dan who, with a bit of embellishment, can sound quite convincing, so long as he's kept well out of the way. He's not really boyfriend material – too geeky for one thing – but when he arrives unexpectedly he turns out to be something of a hero, and quite suitable after all.

Ellie's voice is utterly fresh and convincing, capturing all the intense moments of adolescence. There's the exquisite family boredom – such as a wet holiday in Wales – which contrasts with the warmth and security that only families can give. There's the ever-lurking feeling of being an outsider and, above all, the desperate need to find yourself while conforming with others. Jacqueline Wilson understands all of this; her stories of teenagers are sympathetic and real. Magda and Nadine star in subsequent books in the trilogy, *Girls Under Pressure* and *Girls Out Late*.

Recommended age: 11+

Paul Zindel
The Pigman
Red Fox

John and Lorraine, two alienated American teenagers,
ring up a Mr Angelo Pignati one day on the pretence
that they work for a charity. They pick his name out of
the phone book at random – simply part of a game to
keep those at the other end of the line talking as long as
possible before they realize they are the victims of a
practical joke. But old Mr Pignati, lonely after the death
of his wife, is so glad of a chat that he never suspects
anything is wrong. Inviting the pair over to his house,
he proudly shows them his collection of china pigs.
Nicknaming him 'Mr Pigman' in return, John and
Lorraine end up becoming fond of the nice old man,
with his endless stories, jokes and small acts of
kindness. But under pressure from friends, they take
advantage of Mr Pignati's absence one evening and
throw a party during which his already shabby house is
comprehensively trashed. Overcome with remorse, John
and Lorraine now want to make amends, but have they
left it too late?

First published in 1969, this famous story has lost
none of its freshness in the years since. John and
Lorraine remain two totally believable adolescents,
anti-authority at home and school while over-eager to
keep up with their peer group outside. The character of
Mr Pignati is closely based upon a sweet-natured
Italian grandfather known to the author during his
own unhappy adolescence; an experience he describes

love, sex and change

53

in his moving memoir *The Pigman and Me*. And for
readers who want to read more about John and
Lorraine, there is *The Pigman's Legacy*, also highly
recommended.

Recommended age: 13+

love, sex and change

tough times

J.G. Ballard
Empire of the Sun
Flamingo

Jim, an 11-year-old British
schoolboy, gets separated from
his parents in the chaos
following the Japanese
invasion of Shanghai during
World War II. Left to fend for
himself, he first tries to make
friends with the invading
Japanese army before ending
up with two tough American
adventurers. After a brief spell
in prison, he is sent to a grim
detention centre. There he
sees acts of great cruelty but

because he is still young the Japanese guards mostly leave
him alone. Determined to find his parents, Jim travels
from camp to camp, meeting different British prisoners
on the way. With food getting dangerously short and
clean water hard to find, he only just gets by. Finally
reunited with his parents, who have also been
imprisoned, Jim celebrates the end of the war. But after
all the horrors he has seen, he will never be the same
person again.

This fine novel is closely based on the author's own
childhood experiences in wartime China. Fascinated by
everything around him, Jim never realizes quite how
close to death he often finds himself. While conscious

tough times

of some very bad things happening, he remains curiously detached, almost as if he can't afford to admit the full horror of his situation. Largely ignored by his captors, he even manages to make a few friends among them. Only as he gets older does he begin to understand the true nature of the barbarous evil he has witnessed. This is one of the best novels ever written about the way that war degrades everyone, captors and captured alike.

Recommended age: 15+

Lynne Reid Banks
One More River
Puffin

Lesley was having a good time in Canada, the country where she was born, until the day her Jewish parents announced that the whole family was moving to Israel

to live on a kibbutz. Since this type of communal farm is based on sharing, Lesley will no longer have her own bedroom, and must eat with her own family in the same room as everyone else. She immediately objects, especially when she discovers she will also have to learn Hebrew and that the kibbutz is situated near the border with Jordan – not a safe place to live. But she eventually settles down there, until a secret friendship with an Arab boy throws her life into new turmoil.

Although this story is set in the 1960s, the hatred between many Jews and Arabs it describes has scarcely abated. The author, who lived for nine years on a kibbutz herself, knows the situation well. She also has sympathy for both sides, and tries to suggest ways in which the people involved can still reach out to each other at a personal level. But this is not simply a story with a strong political message. Lynne Reid Banks is also a brilliant writer, expert in bringing out the inevitable tensions arising between teenagers, their parents, and sometimes between them and their best friends. *Secrets and Affairs*, another story set in the same time and place, is also recommended for readers who want to find out more about what it is like to live in this exceptionally troubled part of the world.

Recommended age: 11+

David Belbin
The Last Virgin
Hodder

Six friends, aged somewhere between 15 and 16, look forward to a summer of boys, parties and, for some of them at least, first-time sex. No one is in too much of a hurry, but there is still a keen sense of not wanting to be the last in the group to discover what sex is all about. The various boys who come into the picture range from 'users' like handsome Iain, never without a latest conquest, and nice but insecure lads like Jack, persistently unable to get it quite right. But the girls have their problems, too, unwilling to be labelled as slags, but equally anxious not to be left on the shelf. Parvinder is an exception here, since her parents have already fixed her up with an arranged marriage. So who will finally end up in whose bed? And will they truly feel the better for it?

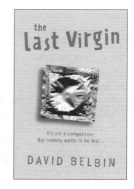

the Last Virgin

It's not a competition
But nobody wants to be last...

DAVID BELBIN

Despite its jokey title, this is not a story that makes fun of adolescents and their quest to explore and understand their maturing sexuality. Anxious not to appear innocent, but not experienced enough to be genuinely worldly-wise, they find it can be a very fraught period of life. Some try to get through it by boasting and general bluster; others attempt a more honest approach. The author considers all such attitudes, always choosing to understand rather than condemn. He has written numerous novels about young adults, but this is his most outspoken. The frank and detailed discussions about sex throughout this sympathetic story are surely welcome at a time when Britain still has the largest number of unplanned teenage births in the whole of western Europe.

Recommended age: 15+

tough times

Malorie Blackman
Noughts and Crosses
Corgi

Noughts are white and Crosses are black; Noughts have nothing, Crosses have everything. Power, education, justice and freedom – there is no equality. Even love cannot transcend the boundaries or break down the barriers. But in *Noughts and Crosses* Malorie Blackman turns such racial stereotypes on their heads with powerful results, breathing fresh life into an age-old story. Sephy and Callum come from opposite sides of the tracks, but they grew up together. Falling in love is so natural – how could it be wrong? Sephy is a Cross: she comes from one of the most powerful families in the country. Her father is high-up in government, and might even be prime minister one day. Callum's family, meanwhile, eke out a living in the slums: he is a Nought. But both are clever and by winning a place at the prestigious Cross school, Callum thinks his education will bring him to her level. But in a society where Crosses and Noughts are hardening their attitudes, breaking conventions is harder than either Sephy or Callum imagined.

Against a background of discrimination and rising tension, Sephy and Callum

tough times

61

struggle to keep going. Malorie Blackman pulls no punches with an uncompromising ending: there is no happy-ever-after. *Noughts and Crosses* is a great love story as well as a stinging commentary on all kinds of racial prejudice.

Recommended age: 11+

Tim Bowler
Midget
Oxford

A passion for sailing and a stubborn streak of self-belief give Midget just enough courage to keep alive his dream; in this exciting battle for survival between two brothers, he triumphs over the adversities of his limited physical condition.

> 66 He scowled down at the body he hated, and thought how good it would be to murder that, if he only knew he could replace it with a decent one. 99

The odds are definitely stacked against 15-year-old Midget: he's only three feet tall, his speech is disjointed and often incoherent, and he suffers from fits. With such handicaps from birth, it's not surprising that Midget seems increasingly unable to cope with anything normal – certainly compared with his handsome and successful older brother, Seb, who always happens to be around just when Midget has his worst attacks, lending a helping hand and keeping him safe. But Midget knows that Seb is the danger. It is he who torments Midget, filling his thoughts with poison under the cover of trying to help him. Seb blames Midget for their mother's death, in particular, and finds every opportunity to accuse Midget of it. Strengthened by the belief of an old man, the care of a nice girl and the advice of a professional psychiatrist, Midget draws on his own courage to fulfil his dream as a sailor and to challenge Seb in a contest which he must win. Midget's story is uplifting as he is freed from his handicaps by his determination.

Recommended age: 13+

Kevin Brooks
Lucas
Chicken House

The first time she sees him Caitlin is fascinated by the solitary Lucas, who arrives from nowhere one afternoon and then sets about fending for himself alone in the remote countryside. While the other boys in the island where she lives tend to be crude and aggressive – including her own older brother – Lucas seems nicer in every way. This soon leads to jealousy and suspicion from the local teenagers, ending up with Lucas accused of a crime when he had in reality behaved with great bravery. An ugly mood develops with the growing threat of violence against Lucas, now pictured by his enemies as a thieving, possibly murderous gypsy. When it seems that Caitlin and her father will also be attacked for sheltering him, Lucas breaks cover in order to divert the rampaging mob's attention.

The image of the romantic outsider coming in to stir up a closed community is an ancient theme in world literature. Sometimes such figures are shown as leading the people they find there towards a better life. At other times, they simply provoke hatred and envy because they expose the local bullies and loudmouths for what they are. Such is the case with Lucas, who wants to be on his own but can't help making a stand against Jamie Tait, the son of the local MP and a nasty piece of work. Caitlin's father tries to help, but is hindered by his hard drinking. Only Caitlin is left to save Lucas, driven on by her first experience of falling in love. Real life may seldom turn out quite as dramatic as this, but with such a well-written, gripping story, who's going to complain?

Recommended age: 13+

Jennifer Choldenko
Notes From a Liar and Her Dog
Bloomsbury

Antonia, commonly known as Ant, is always in big trouble. While her two other sisters are good at home, Ant is always spoiling for a fight. She also has the infuriating habit of telling everyone, including her mother and father, that they are not her real parents. The only lights in her life are Harrison, her best friend, and Pistachio, a tiny dog now getting old, smelly and no longer reliably house-trained. Ant even manages to upset the one teacher who always defends her at school. With vet's bills looming and parents who can't and won't afford them, more trouble looms. How Ant manages to wriggle out of all this and even come out more or less on top is best left to this highly engaging novel to tell for itself.

Although set in the USA, this story could apply to adolescents anywhere who sometimes feel misunderstood. Ant thinks everyone else is to blame; her parents feel they have an unloving daughter who prefers her old dog to them. Working things out between these two positions is not easy, yet when it finally happens the result is extremely moving. Before that, laughter is never far away, simply because Ant is always funny. But behind the humour there is a person who is not particularly happy. Her friendly teacher knows this, and by sticking to Ant – even after her worst episode of bad behaviour at the nearby Zoo Park – she finally helps turn this rebellious girl into someone less self-destructive and a good deal more loveable.

Recommended age: 11+

Brock Cole
The Facts Speak for Themselves
Macmillan

Linda's narrative tells the tragic story of her life, just as she told it to the police officers when they questioned her about Jack's murder. Despite its enormous drama, her retelling is not sensational, allowing readers to

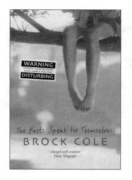

make judgements and decide for themselves who is responsible for what has happened and how truthful Linda's account is. She records what has happened to her, apparently without artifice: what she sees as the facts of her life.

And grim reading they make. From very early on she suffers as a victim of her mother's chaotic lifestyle and repeatedly bad choice of partners. Linda's life is one of poverty, neglect and emotional confusion – all of which make her easy prey when one of those many disreputable men begins a sexual relationship with her. Never having been properly loved, cherished or even made to feel secure, Linda no longer has a sense of what is or isn't appropriate. She can only survive, as well as she can, snatching at what passes for love – or at least attention – because it is to some small degree preferable to coping entirely alone.

Linda's story is an extreme one, but *The Facts Speak for Themselves* is a thought-provoking and chilling reminder of how many children are trapped in lives from which the protection usually afforded by childhood is missing.

Recommended age: 15+

Robert Cormier
The Bumblebee Flies Anyway
Puffin

Barney Snow, who has an incurable illness, volunteers
for treatment at an experimental children's hospital.
There he meets other young people in a similar state,
such as Billy the Kidney, in his wheelchair, Allie Roon,
who is nearly speechless, and Mazzo, already wasting
away from a terrible disease. Receiving no sympathy
from the dictatorial staff working at the hospital, the
four teenagers resolve to perform one last act of
defiance and independence before they die. In total
secrecy they fashion a makeshift plane, known as the
'bumblebee' and created from a sports car. In the
closing pages Mazzo and Billy take up seats in the
plane, triumphantly driving it off the hospital roof with
the satisfaction of having achieved their final aim.

Robert Cormier has always been controversial,
writing tough stories about subjects such as bullying,
terrorism, psychological torture and parental betrayal.
This novel is less realistic than his others, given that no
hospital would ever treat sick young patients in so
heartless a way. But the larger point he makes, about
the necessity of standing up to unjust authority, is
found in all his writing. One of the first authors for
teenagers to describe situations of despair and
hopelessness, he is especially expert at setting a
particular, dark mood and then maintaining it to the
end without ever becoming repetitive.

Recommended age: 13+

tough times

Karen Cushman
The Midwife's Apprentice
Macmillan

Aged between 12 and 13, with no-one knowing or caring about her exact birth date, Alyce lives the life of a beggar. Sleeping in dung-heaps to give her warmth during winter nights, she is regularly bullied by the local children. But when midwife Jane Sharp takes her on as her dogsbody, life gradually improves. Work is still hard and conditions poor, but at least there is now some food in her belly as well as the chance to learn a skill. Yet when her big moment comes, Alyce fails and leaves the village in disgrace. Working in a nearby inn she still dreams of returning, and after a lucky break finally takes up her place as the midwife's acknowledged apprentice.

Set in medieval Britain, this book bubbles with weird and wonderful ideas: from curing fever with snail jelly, to easing the birth process with water in which a murderer has washed his hands. But over and above such glimpses of past superstitions and ancient skills, this is a Cinderella story, with Alyce eventually triumphing both over her enemies and over herself. With only a cat for a companion, she eventually makes good, through her own toughness and intelligence. Books about the past sometimes give too rosy a view of the lives of ordinary people. This one is different: while reading as easily as the best fairy tale, it always keeps close to the facts of what actually happened during a period when life was often short and – for most people – unbelievably tough.

Recommended age: 11+

tough times

Graham Gardner
Inventing Elliot
Orion

Badly bullied at his previous
school, under-sized Elliot is
determined the same thing
shouldn't happen at his next.
But although he manages to
avoid trouble, he soon
becomes aware that there is a
secret reign of violence
presided over by three self-
appointed, senior schoolboy
'guardians'. Rather than
become their target, Elliot is
forced to watch the way they
make other smaller,

vulnerable children utterly miserable. Matters come to
a head when Elliot is told that he has been selected to
become one of the guardians of the future. This
involves not just special training but also choosing
future victims. He has already made friends with one
previous picked-on pupil, and has also become close to
Louise who despises the guardians and all they stand
for. The headmaster, meanwhile, suspects something
bad is going on, and asks Elliot for his help. Will he
dare to tell the truth, and so risk more bullying?

This disturbing story has many parallels with George
Orwell's *Nineteen Eighty-Four*. The three boys who make
up the guardians quote it as their favourite story, missing

tough times

the point that it is actually a condemnation of tyranny. They prefer to copy the ruthless techniques described by Orwell by which an evil few can oppress everyone else. But even when Elliot goes along with the guardians' rules, he is still terrified in case it will be his turn next. Slowly realizing that this is no way to live, it still takes more courage than he seems capable of to make the crucial break. Bullying is always hateful, and this story, based in part on the author's personal experience, describes it in unforgettable detail. It shows how necessary it is to make a stand against all bullying, but how easy it can be to go along with it simply for the sake of a quieter life.

Recommended age: 13+

Rosa Guy
The Friends
Puffin

Although 14-year-old Phyllisia was born in the West Indies, she now finds herself going to school in Harlem, one of the toughest areas of New York City. Her fellow pupils, black like herself, still tease her for speaking with a different accent; they also resent the way she has been better educated, beating her up in the playground on her first day. Teachers are little help, locked in conflict with classes that are perpetually threatening to get out of hand. Phyllisia's parents, while anxious for their daughter, also somehow always seem to make things worse. Her only support comes from Edith, a fellow pupil so poor and badly dressed that Phyllisia is as much embarrassed as pleased by her help. A terrible

ROSA GUY
The Friends

In Harlem you need a friend

tragedy finally brings them together, with Phyllisia deciding to stay on in New York rather than return to the West Indies as her father wishes.

Rosa Guy is a magnificent writer; outspoken and honest. Much of this story is based on her own experience of being orphaned at an early age and then going to work in a factory at the age of 14. While never sentimental about her young characters, she is always on their side when it comes to the prejudice they inevitably encounter from being black, poor and female. There are two more stories in this series: *Ruby*, which focuses on Phyllisia's older sister, and *Edith Jackson*. This has as its main character the brave, shabbily dressed orphan already met in this book, and relates how she refuses to be defeated during the many battles she has to fight, desperately trying to keep what is left of her family together.

Recommended age: 13+

Sonya Hartnett
Thursday's Child
Walker

How childhood seems once you're beyond it is always fascinating, especially when it's as unusual as the Flute

children's – and even more so when the narrator is as perceptive as Harper Flute. Now 21, Harper records her family's struggle for life as the Great Depression grips Australia. Harper watches helplessly as her hapless father descends into alcoholism while the rest of the family struggle to keep going. Always in the background is the shadowy figure of Tin, Harper's brother, who lives in a lair of tunnels which he has built deep under the house. Though mostly unseen, Tin protects the family and ultimately saves them. It's a tough time, but Harper doesn't milk the sentiment. Instead she captures the tiny details, piling them one on top of another so that everything is vivid and affecting.

Sonya Hartnett is superb at describing people, places, states (especially childhood) and atmospheres. She is inventive in using Tin both as a silent saviour and as a metaphor for burrowing into her own childhood and, by extension, all childhoods – which invariably include much that is hidden or obscured. *Thursday's Child* is a highly original book – visionary and deeply moving. Though sad, it is never depressing; an underlying and memorable kindness is always present, particularly in the family's understanding of the strange behaviour of

Tin. The book won the Guardian Children's Fiction Award in 2002.

Recommended age: 13+

Gaye Hiçyilmaz
Girl in Red
Orion

All Frankie knows about the girl he keeps looking at from his window is that she has pale plaits and wears a long, red skirt. But later he discovers that she is a refugee gypsy child called Emilia, who has fled from Romania with her parents after they were persecuted. Unfortunately some of the other people who live on Frankie's tough estate also turn against this family, including his own mother. When an old lady he occasionally helps reveals that she was once happily married to a gypsy, Frankie at last has the chance to learn something accurate about them. By now Emilia is attending his own school, with everyone assuming that Frankie shares his mother's hostile and racist views. In fact he is increasingly fascinated by the girl, but tragedy strikes just as everything seems to be sorting itself out. Emilia is driven away, leaving Frankie alone with a mother he no longer wishes to have anything to do with.

This story makes a strong plea for tolerance and understanding. But it also shows how the personal and the political constantly influence each other. Frankie is drawn towards the mysterious Emilia partly because he knows so little about his own background, given that he never knew his father and can't find out anything about him from his mother. Some of those on his estate who take against the gypsy family are shown to be doing so more because they are angry about the poverty of their own lives. And while Frankie needs his mother, he also finds some of her opinions too horrible to live with. The fact that nothing is easy or straightforward helps to make this story both believable and very moving.

Recommended age: 13+

Susan Hill
I'm the King of the Castle
Penguin

'I didn't want you to come here.' The note is attached to lump of Plasticine dropped in front of Charles Kingshaw on arrival at his new home. Edmund Hooper's warning greeting to Kingshaw is confirmed when they meet face to face: Warings is his house and he wants no one else there. Kingshaw is only there because his mother has taken the job of housekeeper and Hooper is determined to hate him. And to break him.

Without any help from the adults around them – Hooper's lonely widowed father; Kingshaw's weak and needy mother – the two boys are left to their own devices. Hooper's persecution of Kingshaw is systematic and cunning. He is already powerful as the son of the house, and it's a position he exploits to the full. Everything in the house is turned into a source of terror. The room where Hooper's grandfather died, and especially the dusty dead moths in their case in the red room – all of these are used to haunt Kingshaw and to weaken his resistance to Hooper's bullying power. Even outside offers no escape. Kingshaw's friendship with Fielding, a local boy, brings brief respite, but even that cannot stop Hooper. Ultimately and tragically, he wins.

> ❝ Now he would have to go into the copse, or up to the wood. He sighed, looking down from the bedroom window, on to the dull front lawn, He thought, make him go away, make him go. ❞

I'm the King of the Castle is a haunting story of childhood anger, aggression and downright cruelty. For different reasons, both Hooper and Kingshaw are misfits: they are lonely and vulnerable children, unsupported by the adults in their lives, who are remote and cold. The violence between them is primitive, wholly convincing and very, very painful to observe.

Recommended age: 15+

Mary Hooper
(Megan)
Bloomsbury

Megan is only 15 when she discovers that she is five months pregnant. The father is a boy in her own year, nice enough but nothing special to her. So in every way this is the last thing she wants; it is also her exam year, when she had been expected to do well. And Megan

(megan)

MARY HOOPER

had no idea there was a baby on the way until a teacher happened to tell the class one day that it was still possible for girls to have periods while they are pregnant. At last she understands why she had been feeling so strange; it also means a showdown with her ambitious mother. Megan is excluded from school, and the plan is that she should have the baby adopted immediately after birth. But Megan herself has yet to make up her own mind about what she wants.

Do the brackets round the title of this powerful novel symbolize the way that Megan finds herself cut off from her former friends? Or do they stand for pregnancy itself and the way that one body encloses another? Both themes are important, as Megan discovers the pain of no longer joining in ordinary group activities as well as the embarrassment of being gossiped about. But she also feels for the child within her as it starts growing larger and moving around. Two more books, *(Megan)2* and *(Megan)3*, take on her story as a single parent still trying to cope with exams, friends, parents and potential boyfriends. Unsentimental, direct and at all times realistic, these three novels fully deserve to expand their already large readership.

Recommended age: 13+

Lois Keith
A Different Life

Livewire

The problems in Libby's life don't look that bad. Who is she going to sit next to on the Year 10 outing to the seaside? How well is she going to do in her exams? What do the boys in the class think of her? It's what you'd expect of a 15-year-old. But then Libby wakes up with a fever, agonizing pains and no feeling in her legs.

So begins the rest of her life. Libby spends weeks, then months, in hospital. There are tests, treatments and, above all, loads of physiotherapy to try to get her walking. Everyone wants to help; her mum and dad and younger brother do their best to be optimistic; her schoolfriends visit and entertain her; everyone tells her to try. Libby is trying but in the end she has to accept that her legs won't ever work again. Who is she now? And what kind of a life can she live?

A Different Life is not just a refreshingly honest account of adjusting to life with a disability – it's a moving story with touches of humour. Lois Keith holds a steady path between sentimentality and harsh reality, depicting with conviction and honesty Libby and her relationships with

family, friends and professionals as she goes through the ups and downs of her illness, her treatment and her partial recovery. Libby is angry, despairing and finally optimistic, but Barbara – whose attitude to her own disability does most to help – convinces her that she must take control. Libby must move on; only she can determine her own future.

Recommended age: 13+

Benjamin Lebert
Crazy
Puffin

Benjamin Lebert was just 16 when he wrote *Crazy*. Written in the first person, it's the story of his own life, told with absolute accuracy. Benjamin is sent off to a new school – a boarding school, this time. It's his fifth school, the last four having thrown him out for one reason or another. This is a

last desperate attempt by his parents to get him to the required level for maths. Benjamin is resigned but not uncooperative. He's determined to try – though doubtful that this school will succeed where the others have failed.

But there is a difference. Here at Castle Neuseelen

benjamin lebert **CRAZY**
Translated by Carol Brown Janeway

Boarding School, all the boys accept Benjamin for himself, from Benjamin's room-mate Janosch to all the others in the gang – Fat Felix, Skinny Felix, Troy and Little Florian. His paralysed left side and his failure at maths make no difference. Each boy has his own problems and Benjamin soon becomes one of them. They just call him 'Crazy'. No longer an oddball, like any other 16-year-old, Benjamin quickly gets caught up in all the out-of-school activities. With the other boys he smokes out of the windows, bunks off school to go drinking in town, and takes part in the nightly visits to the girls' dormitories – even climbing up fire escapes in the middle of the night, helped by his friends. Through friendship he learns that while he will always be separated by his disability he can also live life to the full and belong. *Crazy* captures teenage life as it really is, and is vibrantly translated by Carol Brown Janeway.

Recommended age: 15+

Harper Lee
To Kill a Mockingbird
Penguin

Set against the sweltering, languid heat of the American South, *To Kill a Mockingbird* is a dramatic and thoughtful story about prejudice versus liberal thinking. Told by Scout, looking back on her childhood, it shows how children's awareness matures and develops and, in this case, how Scout and her younger

tough times

brother Jem change their attitudes to themselves and their neighbours.

> **66** Maycomb was an old town, but it was a tired old town when I first knew it. In rainy weather the streets turned to red slop; grass grew on the sidewalks, the courthouse sagged in the square. **99**

Scout and Jem are brought up their father Atticus, a local lawyer with liberal leanings, after the death of their mother. Their daily life is mostly shaped by Calpurnia, the cook who manages their home in the county town of Maycomb. In many ways, it's a childhood of amazing freedom – Scout and Jem play out with their friend Dill and make up their own imaginary games. But it's also a childhood ruled by conventional thinking. Anyone different is suspect, and racial prejudice is an everyday part of life. As unsuspecting children, Scout and Jem play their part, prankishly tormenting the shadowy Boo Radley, around whom unhealthy rumours have been spun. But theirs is a child's version of the real prejudice of the story. When Atticus defends Thomas Robinson, a Negro accused of rape, the children follow his every move, and defending Atticus himself soon becomes their primary task. It's a steep learning curve for Scout and Jem, and one that makes them rethink the substance of their own lives. *To Kill a Mockingbird* has rightly become a classic for its portrayal of an individual speaking out against unthinking racism.

Recommended age: 13+

tough times

Nicola Morgan
Mondays Are Red
Hodder

Waking from a long coma after a serious attack of meningitis, Luke knows immediately that something is very wrong. Sitting in the top right-hand corner of his vision, where only Luke can see him, is a hideous little figure who introduces himself as Dreeg and who promises all sorts of exciting things. Luke's imagination has now become so vivid that music and other sounds can be tasted, and every day of the week possesses its own peculiar colour. As Luke tries to get better through the exercises recommended by the hospital, Dreeg does nothing but sneer. Luke finally realises that this imp is the residue of his illness, and in order to get better he must defeat the nagging voice in his head that is forever rubbishing his best efforts to recover. Dreeg also encourages Luke to commit a fearful crime against his – admittedly detestable – older sister Laura.

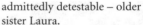

Luke is in fact suffering from synaesthesia – a condition of heightened sensitivity where sound, touch, hearing and vision often become mixed up with each other. No two people experience it in the same way, and it is possible that all babies are born with it, so explaining why memories of early childhood are often so intense and difficult to put into words. In Luke's struggle to get better his illness takes on all the most negative sides of his own personality in the shape of the repulsive Dreeg. Luke's hardest task is his decision to reject the perfect girlfriend Dreeg fashions for him in favour of life as it really is. *Mondays Are Red* is an unusual, fascinating and at times disturbing story, but it is also extremely well written and deserves to be read.

Recommended age: 13+

Sylvia Plath
The Bell Jar
Faber

Having won a fashion magazine contest, Esther and eleven other young college girls now have an all-

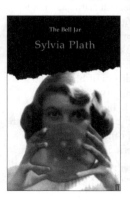

expenses-paid month in New York. The work isn't hard and the advantages are many, but Esther is not enjoying herself. The arrival of her boyfriend Buddy Willard, intent on marriage, does nothing to lift her mood. Gradually Esther feels herself increasingly detached from everything and everyone until she makes a suicide attempt which nearly comes off. After that there is a long spell in mental hospital where she suffers crude, electric-shock treatment before being rescued by a kind benefactor and sent to a more sensitive institution. There Esther slowly recovers, until 'patched, retreaded and approved for the road', she is allowed to leave and once again take up her studies.

> ❝ It was a queer, sultry summer, the summer they electrocuted the Rosenbergs, and I didn't know what I was doing in New York. ❞

This intensely autobiographical account was first published under an assumed name, so as not to upset the author's mother, who makes frequent appearances. Surprisingly funny at times, as well as deeply moving, *The Bell Jar* is one of the best descriptions ever written of what happens when someone can no longer cope with the realities of everyday living. With a poet's eye, the author writes unforgettably about the different ways in which the normal comes to seem abnormal. The personalities she meets on this strange inner journey are equally memorable, all invested with her own, unique sense of meaning. Sylvia Plath killed herself the year this book appeared in 1963, by which time she was already acknowledged as a leading poet. Readers who find themselves caught up in this unforgettable story might also try her fine collection of poems *Ariel,* published two years after her death.

Recommended age: 15+

tough times

Bali Rai
(Un)arranged Marriage
Doubleday

Manny is determined that he'll never succumb to the arranged marriage that his parents have planned for him. To be fixed up with a bride he has never met runs against everything his upbringing in Leicester has taught him. Everything, that is, outside the family.

Manny lives in two worlds. There's the streetwise, cool-dude life of his Leicester schoolfriends – skipping school, smoking, and occasionally shoplifting – and the narrow-minded expectations of his family, expectations that are physically hammered home by Manny's dominating father, whose views are backed up by two equally narrow-minded older brothers. But Manny's family is as just as determined as Manny himself. He is taken to India to learn respect and a proper sense of where he belongs. From this, Manny does get a better perspective on what being a Punjabi really means, but he still rejects the expectations and pressures put upon him. Returning to Britain, Manny finds that his only escape is to give up his family completely and make a new life of his own, so that he can take his own decisions about his future.

With a sharply observant eye for contemporary life, Bali Rai gives an uncompromisingly honest account of the problems of assimilation and cultural conflict. While condemning some aspects of the Punjabi lifestyle in Manny's own family, especially their support for arranged marriages – refreshingly, here seen from a male point of view – Rai also shows the supportive qualities of close family life and the ambitious aspirations of other Punjabis.

Recommended age: 13+

Louis Sachar
Holes
Bloomsbury

A hole a day, five-foot deep, five-foot across – that's what the boys at Camp Green Lake have to dig. Why? Because it's character-building, they are told. But this is no ordinary camp. Far from being the holiday paradise that its name suggests, Camp Green Lake is a detention centre for bad boys set in the middle of the Texan desert. Stanley Yelnats ends up at Camp Green Lake by mistake, wrongly accused of stealing a pair of sneakers. Gradually he adjusts to life at the camp, digging his first holes with help from the boys in his tent.

tough times

Teamwork is important in a place like Camp Green Lake. Gradually, too, Stanley realizes that there must be a reason for these holes and the Warden – a ferocious lady with blood-red nails laced with rattlesnake venom – knows what it is. Through digging his holes, Stanley digs up the truth, piecing it together on a brave journey of discovery with his friend Zero.

> **There is no lake at Camp Green Lake. There was once a very large lake here, the largest lake in Texas. That was over a hundred years ago. Now it is just a dry flat wasteland.**

Sparely written with a lot of delicate humour, and with much left to the imagination, *Holes* is an exceptional book of great humanity and warmth. The searing heat of the desert makes survival the most important issue, and the boys in Camp Green Lake are survivors – showing their enormous courage against great injustice.

Recommended age: 11+

Nicky Singer
Feather Boy
Collins

Twelve-year-old Robert is the class victim at school – bad at games, naturally solitary and easily bullied. So when he volunteers to join a project involving a local Rest Home for the elderly, this becomes one more reason for other pupils to tease him. But Robert meets

Edith Sorrel, an old lady who insists he visits the house where she once lived. This is not an errand he welcomes, since legend has it that a boy once fell to his death there from an upper window. But he feels he has to go when challenged to do so by his chief tormentor Jonathan Niker, who also agrees to come. That night Robert finds the courage first to

stand up to Niker and then to fulfil a promise he makes to Mrs Sorrel which eventually changes both their lives for the better.

> **And I thank the chance that led me, one day, to a huge, derelict house in downtown Hove and the powerful feeling that I just had to go in…**

This story was written after the author's son asked her to write something for his particular age group. The result is a book packed with smart remarks, occasional moments of fear, first serious feeling for the opposite sex and a climax where everything eventually comes good. The moments when Robert is bullied will strike a chord with many readers. This is not just because of the verbal and physical cruelty involved but also because Robert himself no longer bothers to stick up for

tough times

himself – something that often happens in real life. The problem therefore is not just with those who bully him but also with the way that Robert has become used to it. Learning to fight back, as he does in the final chapters, gives this strongly satisfying story just the type of ending its readers would wish for.

Recommended age: 11+

John Steinbeck
Of Mice and Men
Penguin

Full of compassion for the state of the dispossessed, John Steinbeck's *Of Mice and Men* highlights the plight of the migrant workers in the United States during the Great Depression of the 1930s. He set it near his own home in Salinas Valley, California, where he had seen

for himself what happened to the men without work. It is a tragic story of how poverty and need affect people's behaviour.

Like millions of others, George and Lennie, two loners who have nothing much going for them, set out to fulfil the deeply ingrained American dream – to own land of their own. George will take care of things while

tough times

Lennie, who is large but simple-minded, will fulfil his one ambition of raising rabbits. George looks after Lennie as they travel south, protecting him when things go wrong and extracting him from the difficulties which he unintentionally gets into. Finally, pitching up at a farm where they are offered work gives them a glimmer of hope. Settling down, they mix with other workers and Lennie is even given a puppy. But they make enemies, too. Lennie is too vulnerable to cope with the naked anger of Curley and the dangerous advances of his wife. Soon things start to go wrong and Lennie finds himself at the centre of one disaster, then another. George can no longer protect Lennie; he takes what he sees as the only course of action to help him. The shocking ending confirms the tragedy of George and Lennie, whose friendship and sense of fragility inspire Steinbeck's masterpiece.

Recommended age: 15+

Robert Swindells
Stone Cold
Puffin

Life is tough for Link: things at home deteriorate pretty fast after his dad leaves, his mum's new boyfriend Vince is on his case most of the time and, after one drunken night, he locks Link out. Endlessly cold and tired, Link drifts around Bradford for a while before moving to London, where at least there's anonymity and a degree of acceptance of the homeless. But London is

tough times

89

frightening. Link copes only because he is befriended by Ginger, who knows all the tricks of survival. Then Ginger disappears. Link is in despair. What's worse is that other street kids are disappearing too. Who will be next? Could it be Link?

Bitter and violent, a man calling himself 'Shelter' is also on the streets, but he has a mission: to clear up the human garbage, tidy away the sponging, dirty characters who loiter in shop doorways and round the Underground stations. Leaving nothing to chance, he's precise, stalking his targets without pity.

Link and Shelter – each tells his own story, creating a chilling picture of life on the streets. Published in 1993 just as homelessness became a particularly urgent issue, *Stone Cold* is an acid commentary on the subject, and one which demonstrates just how little help is available. Robert Swindells shows compassion for the homeless – without ever sentimentalizing their plight – while writing a gripping thriller with a killer who'll stop at nothing.

Recommended age: 11+

Martin Waddell

Tango's Baby
Walker

Brian Tangello, known to his mates as 'Tango', is aged 16, six-foot-tall, thin as a rake and when he walks looks like a shambling fork-lift truck. He is seen by most – including 14-year-old Crystal O'Leary, the girl he fancies – as one of life's losers. But when he offers

Crystal a shoulder to cry on one night, she warms to him. When Crystal later becomes pregnant, Tango is delighted at the news. After hearing that Crystal's mum is arranging an abortion, the young people run away, first to a hotel and then, when their funds run out, to an unoccupied beach hut. Eventually Crystal, now seven months pregnant, tired and cold, makes her way back home. After many more complications, she rejects Tango for someone else. Utterly distraught, Tango tries snatching back the baby, and ends up in prison.

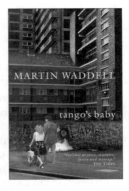

Tango is a vivid example of the sort of pupil forever blamed at school or by society for not behaving in a more sensible way. But this novel shows how such people can also have their own deep feelings, principles and sensitivities. Tango is in fact a born romantic, wanting the best for those he loves but with no idea of how to provide it. Yet despite his occasional troubles with the police and his inability to find or hold down a job, he is not a bad person. This story, narrated as if by one of Tango's few friends, gives a vivid picture of life in an environment where poverty makes it hard for anyone to live a satisfying life, especially someone with such high ideals and low delivery skills as Tango.

Recommended age: 13+

tough times

Alice Walker
The Color Purple
The Women's Press

The Color Purple was an immediate bestseller when it
was published in 1982. Written in a diary form as Celie's
letters to God, it is an astonishing account of survival
and emotional growth from the most desperate
beginnings in the Deep South of America. Celie is only
14 when she begins her diary. She has already been
repeatedly raped by her father, by whom she has had a
couple of babies – both of which he has got rid of. Her
one ambition is to save her pretty and clever younger
sister Nettie from their father, but soon she is traded in
marriage by her father to 'Mister', who abuses her
physically and emotionally – a situation she outwardly
accepts while maintaining the inner strength that she
needs to keep going. Remarkably, the change for Celie
comes when she meets Shug, a confident young singer
whom Mister adores and shamelessly brings home.
Gradually Celie finds herself falling in love with Shug,
whose confidence, success and sheer ability to survive
give Celie enormous courage. Through Shug, Celie
escapes from years of oppression and becomes free. She
gains the confidence she needs to challenge Mister,
which leads her to finding the letters from Nettie which
she has so longed for and which he had hidden.

Celie, Nettie, Shug and all the other women in *The
Color Purple* share experiences of oppression which
bond them, even across the familiar divide of racism.
Their mutual support suffuses their experience,

making this a story of warmth, love and even some happiness.

Recommended age: 15+

Jacqueline Wilson
Dustbin Baby
Corgi

Fourteen-year-old April hates the fact that her birthday is on April 1. This, and her habit of frequently bursting into tears, give the other children in her class the idea for her nickname, 'April Showers'. But April would rather be called that than 'Dustbin Baby', a reference to the fact that as a new-born baby she was rescued by a student from the refuse bin where she had been abandoned.

Now living with her long-suffering foster mother Marion, April finds herself continually thinking about her past life, including a disastrous period where she was first adopted and then rejected by a married couple who were in the process of breaking up. After her adopted mother finally committed suicide, April was sent to a number of care placements, none of which worked out. No wonder she cries so much when thinking about her past. But there is still one more surprise yet to come.

tough times

> **Funny kind of cradle. A pizza box for a pillow, newspaper for a coverlet, scrunched-up tissues serving as a mattress. What kind of mother could dump her own baby in a dustbin?**

Jacqueline Wilson is expert in describing teenagers who often seem a nuisance to others because they have such difficulty in coming to terms with what they have missed out on in their own lives. But she is also brilliant at creating equally believable characters who want to help them, in this case the saintly Marion. Marion needs to be loved, too, and has the patience to wait until April has finally finished with her fantasy of being reunited with the mother who abandoned her. April does get to meet the person who rescued her, and by talking to him realises how much she depends on the security and unconditional love offered to her by Marion. This is a book to make you cry as well as laugh, and it's never less than totally engrossing.

Recommended age: 11+

Virginia Euwer Wolff
True Believer
Faber

LaVaughn is 15 and finding life hard. Her mother is distracted by a new man, school is not going well and she is increasingly aware of the poverty of the surroundings where she and the rest of her family live. And while she does not want to give herself away to the first local boy, she hates being alone when it comes to Saturday night. Then Jody arrives on the scene – upright, handsome and well-mannered. Their first kiss is everything LaVaughn has ever dreamed about, but something still isn't right.

Readers of the same author's *Make Lemonade* will already be familiar with LaVaughn and the way she helped out Jolly, a young, unmarried mother only a few years older than herself. Jolly also turns up in this story, but the focus is now firmly on LaVaughn herself, and her unease at the way some of her friends seem to be going wrong. She is also unsure about her mother's new man, and very harsh on the one boy in her class at school who keeps trying to impress her. Told in the form of a long prose-poem, this story reads easily and has a compelling immediacy.

Recommended age: 13+

Benjamin Zephaniah
Refugee Boy
Bloomsbury

Alem's father is Ethiopian but his mother is Eritrean. When these countries go to war, his parents are seen as traitors by both sides. Arriving in London as a refugee, Alem wakes up next morning to discover his father has returned to Africa to try and help end the civil war. Entirely on his own, Alem is sent to a children's home, but when this proves too tough he is placed with foster parents and starts attending school. He then learns that

tough times

refugee boy
benjamin zephaniah

From the best-selling
author of FACE

his mother has been killed and that he may be expelled from Britain because of problems with his application to seek asylum. But at least Alem is reunited with his father, over in Britain again. When local people hear that father and son may be deported they put on a Freedom Dance to raise funds for their appeal. Things seem to be going well, but more troubles are on the way.

Much of this novel is taken up with the actual details of what currently happens to people seeking asylum in Britain. Alem's view of Britain as an outsider is always fascinating and sometimes even comic. The other asylum seekers he meets all have their own, frequently tragic stories to tell, but although the book is often unavoidably sad, it is still in many ways a feel-good story. Alem is the sort of positive character who brings out the best in others as well as in himself. To read this novel is to become better informed about a controversial topic where there are no easy answers.

Recommended age: 11+

tough times

in danger

David Almond
Kit's Wilderness

Hodder

At the age of 13, Kit goes with his parents to help look after his elderly grandfather. His new home is a town in the northeast of England where generations of men – including his grandfather – have worked in the mines. Now, there's nothing left of the industry except a pock-marked landscape which, with its secret chambers, provides a fascinating and dangerous attraction that is irresistible to children. It is here

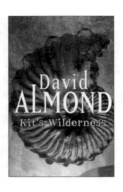

that Kit joins with the others in the scary 'game of death' which forms part of a ritual of belonging. It's a tense and dangerous activity that leads to Kit's involvement with a mysterious and wild boy named John Askew. Gradually Kit becomes aware that the whole area is haunted by the memory of a dreadful mining accident in the past. His grandfather knows something about it, and so too does a mysterious presence that seems to light Kit's way when he becomes trapped underground. David Almond is a subtle and understated writer, and *Kit's Wilderness* is an enormously thought-provoking book in which the boundaries between reality, memory and imagination are often disturbingly blurred.

Recommended age: 13+

in danger

Melvin Burgess
Junk
Puffin

Gemma is friendly with Tar,
who is having a tough time at
home with a father who lays
into him after secret drinking
sessions. He finally runs away,
and Gemma joins him in a
squat. For a while all goes well
until other young squatters
introduce them to hard drugs.
Under the impression they are
just experimenting, Gemma
and Tar are gradually drawn
into total dependency before

they realize what is happening. Petty crime and
prostitution follow, until Gemma – now in hospital – is
reunited with her parents. At 18 years old she looks so
old and wasted that they barely recognize her.

There have been other novels about young people
and addiction, but this was the first to show why hard
drugs can seem so attractive. Tar and Gemma begin by
finding heroin a totally pleasant experience, enabling
them to forget their worries and just float away. They
think they can give it up at any time, but when they
finally try, it is not so easy. To make matters worse,
everyone in their squat is quarrelling – the drug makes
them mean as well as needy. They are all deteriorating
physically, too, feeling permanently sick and forever

searching for new veins to inject. Told from the point of view of several different characters, this story is hard-hitting but completely gripping. The author writes in his preface that 'This book isn't fact…it's all true, every word.' It deserves to be read by as many young people as possible.

Recommended age: 15+

Albert Camus
The Outsider
Penguin

Meursault is a young Frenchman working in Algiers. Selfish and generally laid-back, he suffers no obvious grief when his mother dies, finding her funeral more embarrassing than moving. He has little respect for anyone who is not also young and pleasure-seeking like himself, and he gets on particularly well with Raymond, a neighbour with a taste for low life and violence. A walk on the beach with him leads to a pointless fight with a couple of Arabs. First knives and then revolvers come into play as Meursault, for no obvious reason, finishes by shooting one of the Arabs dead. Arrested and tried, he refuses to defend himself. Sentenced to death, his only reaction is to feel glad he is going to die now in his prime rather than having to wait for an undignified old age to carry him off years later.

Albert Camus was a philosopher as well as a writer (he was also a talented footballer). In this short novel he describes an individual forever on the fringes of

in danger

what is going on. Witnessing others pretending to have the feelings expected of them by the rest of society, he has no intention of playing any such games himself. He is therefore quite honest when he tells the court that he does not know why exactly he killed a man except that the blazing sun had been particularly bothering him at the time. As always, he comes over as a man who lives for nothing except for himself and his few friends. Is Meursault really different from the rest of humankind? Or is he simply more honest? Readers will have to decide this question for themselves after finishing this strange story, written by one of the great authors of the twentieth century.

Recommended age: 15+

Joseph Conrad
Heart of Darkness
Penguin

Waiting aboard his yacht for the tide to turn in the Thames Estuary, Marlow tells his four companions the story of a terrible journey he once made to Africa. As captain of a steamer collecting ivory from different trading posts on the Congo River, he had come to hear about a certain Mr Kurtz. This man was not only a most effective ivory trader; he also had a reputation for treating the local population with fairness and compassion. Such qualities were rare at the time, when corrupt and greedy white traders often looked on the natives of the area as their slaves. Marlow sets out to find Kurtz, after hearing that he is seriously ill. But

Joseph Conrad Heart of Darkness

when they finally meet, he discovers that Kurtz has become a depraved local ruler, living in a sordid hut surrounded by posts decorated with human heads. Back on the boat, Kurtz eventually dies, his last cry still ringing in Marlow's ears: 'The horror! The horror!'

Written in densely constructed prose, this short novel is a masterpiece in what it suggests as well as says. While it is never certain what exactly Kurtz got up to in the jungle, the atmosphere of evil finally surrounding him is unmistakeable. But this evil is found not just within individuals, but in the whole, sick enterprise by which white adventurers – under the guise of colonialism – raided Africa for what they could get from it. Marlow is disgusted by what he sees, but he is also intrigued by Kurtz. Was his fall all the greater because he had once actually tried to do some good, only to be eventually defeated by the cruelty inherent within imperialism? First published in 1902, this unforgettable story later formed the basis for the film *Apocalypse Now,* with the main action moved to the Vietnam War during the 1960s.

Recommended age: 15+

in danger

Peter Dickinson
AK

Macmillan

Paul Kagomi is a boy soldier. All his life he has been fighting in the African bush. With no parents that he can remember, he has been looked after by Michael, one of the leading warriors in the Fifth Special Commando of the Nagala Liberation Army and the man designated to be his uncle. In a life of uncertainty, the only securities Paul knows are Michael, and his beloved

AK47 assault rifle. But then peace comes, and Paul is sent off to school – although not before he has buried his AK for safe-keeping. It's a shrewd move as the peace is fragile. When the new government falls, soldiers come to burn the school and kill the children, and Paul is on the run once again. He escapes the carnage with a group of friends and flees into the bush for safety. But hiding out is never a lasting option and Paul knows that before anything else he must retrieve his rifle: it's the only thing he can completely rely on. A man's gun in a boy's hands, it gives Paul what he needs to survive.

The story of Paul's resilience in an unstable country, where cycles of war and peace seem impossible to break, is both thrilling and poignant. There are no false heroics, but Peter Dickinson's characters emerge as tough and brave individuals.

Recommended age: 11+

Alan Gibbons
Caught in the Crossfire

Orion

Oakfield is a depressed northern town with a large population of British Muslims. Everyone gets on reasonably well there until the arrival of John Creed and his new, Nazi-style political party, the Patriotic League. In his search for recruits, Creed soon manages to stoke up racial tension by skilfully distorting the truth to his own advantage. The effects of his intervention are soon evident. The Kelly family is torn apart when principled 17-year-old Mike feuds with Creed's latest recruit, his own younger brother Liam. The Khan family is also having a tough time, with fiery Tahir determined to fight back even when his twin sister Rabia is convinced he is setting about things in the wrong way. Mike and Rabia finally fall for each other, but will their love be enough to defeat the forces of hate surrounding them on both sides?

Books written specifically to make a political point don't always come off, but there is still enough driving force in this story to carry readers through to its explosive climax. Its characters are not particularly memorable, but the events they are caught up in have a

in danger

105

nightmare quality all the more disturbing for their closeness to what has actually happened in race riots within Britain.

Recommended age: 11+

William Golding
Lord of the Flies
Faber

A party of pre-teenage schoolboys is marooned after their plane crashes on a desert island. Without any accompanying adults, they have to fend for themselves. Ralph is voted leader, but his authority is soon challenged by Jack, a power-hungry rival. Things deteriorate as Jack, now in charge of a group of pig-hunters, gradually isolates Ralph and his intelligent but unpopular friend known to everyone as Piggy because

he is fat. Ralph desperately tries to keep a permanent fire going as a signal to passing boats that the children are there. But Jack and his gang – now covered in war paint and brandishing home-made spears – eventually turn on Ralph and his few remaining friends. The ensuing mayhem ends only with the unexpected arrival of a British naval officer.

in danger

106

Many stories have been written about what life might be like on a desert island, usually stressing the joys of total independence. This book takes a different view, arguing that in such a situation young humans, without the support of family and society, would soon revert to barbarism. William Golding, who wrote *Lord of the Flies* shortly after the end of World War II, believed that evil could be found anywhere in the world – not simply in Germany and Japan, the enemy countries of the time.

> **With the boar only five yards away, he flung the foolish wooden stick that he carried, saw it hit the great snout and hang there for a moment. The boar's note changed to a squeal and it swerved aside into the covert.**

Few novels have stirred as much debate as this. Would the situation have been different if girls had been there too? Might a different group of children, perhaps from a less competitive type of culture, have made a better job of living on the island? Though written for adults, this book has since proved equally popular with younger readers, not least because of the questions it raises about what it means to be human. It is also an expert example of storytelling that never lets up on the tension from first page to last.

Recommended age: 15+

in danger

Keith Gray
Warehouse
Red Fox

Robbie, Canner, Lem, Selly, Kinnard and Amy have one thing in common: they all live in the Warehouse. Their reasons for being there are all different but, along with many others, they find shelter in the one place where few questions are asked, where you can be yourself and where you can be safe. For Robbie, safety comes first; anywhere away from his brother is good. For Amy, it's a temporary haven where she can escape from other people's expectations of her. For Canner and Lem, it's the only life they want to know. Reaching back into their own pasts is too painful, though Lem's strict no-drugs rule has its origins in his own experience. Together they rule the Warehouse, guiding the others. But despite their best efforts, even that isn't safe for ever. Ultimately, there is no safety, only survival and friendship.

Keith Gray looks behind the surface of homelessness and dispossession. He looks at the many different reasons why so many step, or fall, out of conventional society and find themselves living on the margins. Above all, he writes with compassion and intelligence

in danger

about an alternative way of life that, despite appearances, has its own rules and clearly defined morality. The result is that *Warehouse* is a book of enormous hope.

Recommended age: 13+

Reinhardt Jung
Dreaming in Black and White
Mammoth

Hannes Keller lives in modern Germany. He was born disabled and walks with a crutch, which creates problems particularly with his father, who is ashamed to have a son who is different from others. Hannes also has the most troubling dreams, where he goes back over sixty years to a time in Germany when the Nazi party was in power. Still disabled, he finds that those then in power would like him and other disabled people to be put to death under the guise of giving them 'treatment'. The fact that Hannes is a bright pupil counts for little; as with the Jewish pupils in his class, there is simply no room for them in the Germany of that time. Back in the present, Hannes wonders whether disabled children like himself will be

in danger

allowed to survive much longer in modern times now that the genetic screening of unborn babies has become such an increasingly exact science.

> ❝ **I used to be sorry I couldn't get back into my dreams. Now I'm afraid of what's sure to happen next.** ❞

This is a short book, fewer than a hundred pages long. But it provides an unforgettable picture of Nazi Germany and the way that intolerance was encouraged as part of the political system. It now seems shocking to victimize the disabled, but the author does not allow readers the comfort of feeling that things are that much better today. The disabled still often find themselves on the fringes of society, with no proper provision for leading an independent life. *Dreaming in Black and White* is the kind of book that can challenge attitudes and even change the way that people think.

Recommended age: 15+

Ken Kesey
One Flew Over the Cuckoo's Nest
Macmillan

Set in a mental institution, *One Flew Over the Cuckoo's Nest* is narrated by one of the inmates, Chief Bromden, who is – apparently – in a permanent catatonic state and both deaf and dumb. The chief sees everything that goes on, although his understanding is incomplete since he also suffers from hallucinations. His life, and those of

in danger

other patients such as Dale Harding and Billy Babbit, is controlled by the all-powerful Nurse Ratched, who can summon up medical or physical reinforcements at any time. But everything changes with the arrival of Randall Patrick McMurphy who challenges Nurse Ratched and the doctors at the institution, questioning the treatment of the patients and encouraging them to break out of the

physical and mental prison they have been put into. Unlike the others, McMurphy refuses to accept that he is mad while the doctors and nurses are sane. Instead he tries to find out what it going on, stumbling across the institution's final solution to 'problem' patients – lobotomy. At first, McMurphy's subversive tactics are exhilarating and liberating but gradually everything gets out of control and the consequences are horrifying.

One Flew Over the Cuckoo's Nest is a novel that challenges preconceptions about madness and its treatment. Through the character of McMurphy, Ken Kesey shows how people are often defined as mentally ill and then trapped by treatments which may, in fact, be making them worse. This disturbing book, which was made into a powerful Hollywood film, offers no simple answers to the questions it raises.

Recommended age: 15+

in danger

Henning Mankell
Secrets in the Fire

Allen & Unwin

A story of almost unbearable pain tempered by amazing courage and kindness, *Secrets in the Fire* tells of the all-too-real horror of war and poverty in general, and the devastation caused by land mines in particular. Set in Mozambique, where the hidden legacy of years of civil war lies buried in the ground, the people of the villages eke out a living, surviving – against all odds – both extreme poverty and endless violence. When bandits kill her father, Sofia flees her village with her beloved sister, mother and younger brother, and attempt to build a new life. Sofia and Maria help their mother in the fields and even go to school. Like everyone else, they take care because there are landmines everywhere. They know they must keep to the paths. But one joyous, unsuspecting leap off the track proves to be a fatal mistake: Maria is killed and Sofia loses her legs. Her rehabilitation is a long one: stuck in a hospital far away from home, she learns to walk again with artificial legs and, helped by the kindness of strangers, she eventually comes to terms with the loss of her sister and her childhood.

Henning Mankell's simple, unsentimental writing describes the way individuals and whole societies learn to cope with violence, poverty and death. Based on the true story of a remarkable young girl, *Secrets in the Fire* is both a wonderful account and an important insight into the lives of others.

Recommended age: 13+

in danger

Beverley Naidoo
The Other Side of Truth
Puffin

It's early morning and Sade is packing her schoolbag when two shots ring out. With those shots, her world changes. After her mother's death – killed as a reprisal because of a controversial article by her father – Sade, and her sister Femi, have to make a new start. They must leave Nigeria, quickly and in secret. It's scary but at least they'll be safe, staying with their uncle in Britain. But things don't go according to plan. Abandoned with no money by their courier in a London that is cold, wet and frightening, Sade and Femi discover just how difficult it is to survive in a country that is hostile and suspicious of newcomers. They haven't got the right papers, no one knows what to do with them and, above all, they don't know what answers to give. Sade has to think hard and fast to make sure she and Femi stay together and that their father can find them. Sade's courage and intelligence help her through, and fortunately there are kind adults as well as those who make things difficult.

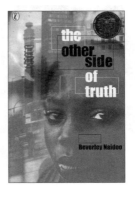

The Other Side of Truth kindles a desire for justice, freedom and humanity: it portrays an accurate picture

in danger

of the way in which some people are forced to flee their own countries, the complications of cultural misunderstanding when they arrive as well the obstacles that are put in their way. Reading it will change perceptions – even if it cannot provide answers.

Recommended age: 11+

Gudrun Pausewang
The Final Journey
Puffin

'The sliding door of the railway truck closed with a deafening clang.' So begins what 11-year-old Alice does not yet know will be the final journey of her life. In the company of her grandfather, she and other Jews living in Germany are being transported to an unknown destination. Her grandmother has already

disappeared, and her parents have also been taken away. As the cattle trucks trundle towards the East, conditions get worse by the hour. Deprived of water and food and with no toilets, some passengers really begin to suffer. Alice herself sees more horror in three days than she has ever experienced in a whole lifetime. But she still looks forward to the end of

in danger

the journey and a cleansing shower to wash all the grime away.

What Alice and the other travellers do not know is that when they finally arrive at the concentration camp most of them will be gassed to death in the very showers they think are there for the purposes of getting them clean. As law-abiding citizens, some of whose parents had fought for Germany in World War I, they can't conceive the level of hatred that would condemn them to death simply because of their race.

Sparely told, and written with compassion rather than with a crude desire to shock, this story is based on the real experience of thousands of adults and children between 1939 and 1945. Reading it now is inevitably a disturbing and depressing experience. But it is also a story that should be known, in order to try to make sure that such horrors never happen again.

Recommended age: 13+

Alexander Solzhenitsyn
One Day in the Life of Ivan Denisovich
Penguin

It's 5am, time for Ivan to get up in the freezing barrack room where he is imprisoned along with other so-called 'enemies of the Soviet Union'. Before he starts his labouring work in the freezing Siberian ice and snow, there are other tasks to do: sewing extra material into his ragged clothes to make them a bit warmer; carrying and fetching for any prisoner who still has

in danger

money to spare; collecting breakfast bowls from the kitchen with the off-chance of getting an extra bite to eat. Ivan employs the various tactics he has learned in order to survive the inadequate food, back-breaking work and the casual cruelties of the bored guards. There are occasional conversations with other prisoners, such as Alyosha who has been arrested for his Christian beliefs, but Ivan is mostly concerned simply with surviving each day as best he can.

Published in 1962, *One Day in the Life of Ivan Denisovich* was one of the first novels to write honestly about the appalling cruelties that were common in communist Russia. The author drew on his own eight years in a labour camp, where he was imprisoned for making critical remarks about the Russian dictator Stalin. His short book is written from the point of view of one quite ordinary man, who stands for the many thousands of Russian citizens who were locked away during those dark times. While not a hero, there is something heroic in Ivan's determination to get by in such inhuman conditions.

Recommended age: 15+

in danger

Mildred Taylor
Roll of Thunder, Hear My Cry
Puffin

Set in the cotton-growing farmlands of the Mississippi Delta almost a century ago, *Roll of Thunder, Hear My Cry* contrasts the strength and warmth of a black family with the chilling hatred and violence that surrounds them. White supremacy permeates every aspect of life, from the inequalities of the education system to the corruption that governs even the most basic needs. Cassie's mother tries to instil a fierce sense of pride into her children, and Cassie especially, as they struggle against the deep-seated racism they face at every turn. While her parents accept, submit and make sacrifices, Cassie and the rest of her generation square up to the unfairness. Cassie asks questions that demand urgent answers, especially as the tension rises and violence erupts. Through Cassie's eyes, and drawing on her own family history, Mildred Taylor conveys the ways in which – despite the ending of slavery – whites continued to control blacks through intimidation.

Recommended age: 11+

in danger

James Watson
Talking in Whispers
Puffin

Sixteen-year-old Andres's life is changed for ever when he sees his father arrested and his best friend killed by the military police. Barely escaping with his life, Andres is now a wanted man but he is also determined to find his father and to devote his life to fighting against the dictatorship that rules his country. Set in Chile after the worst years of the Pinochet regime, *Talking in Whispers* is the story of how ordinary people, and young people in particular, can fight for freedom and justice. Andres makes friends with Isa and her twin brother Beto, who are also searching for relatives who have disappeared. Together they take unimaginable risks in standing up to the authorities, for, as Isa says, 'after a while you come to hate talking in whispers'. But, with the secret police everywhere, it's hard to know whom to trust. Arrest would lead to incarceration in the ill-named House of Laughter, a place from which few return.

A fast-paced political thriller, in which there is real danger – including some gruesome descriptions of torture – *Talking in Whispers* is also an inspiring story of the value of democracy and the need to fight for it, highlighting the plight of those who live under political oppression.

Recommended age: 15+

in danger

crime

Iain Banks
The Crow Road
Abacus

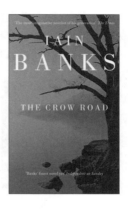

Warm, authentic, gripping and, above all, very funny, *The Crow Road* is a vast family saga as well as the story of its narrator's own journey of discovery. A disorganized yet questioning student, drinking, sleeping and dabbling in drugs and sex when he can, Keith McHoan divides his time between his chaotic student life and his family. When at home, he tries to unravel some of the complicated and interconnected stories of his friends and relatives – especially the mysterious disappearance of his uncle Rory. Family myths, sibling rivalry, the particular role of old friends, the deceits practised by adults on children, and the naive and partial view of the world which children have – these are all woven into Keith's story of growing up and into his greater understanding of himself. *The Crow Road* is a novel that points up the similarities between different generations, with the story moving easily between them, and shows how what happens in the past can also affect the present, often in a profound way.

Recommended age: 15+

crime

Raymond Chandler

The Big Sleep

Penguin

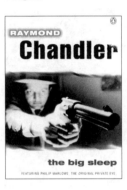

Philip Marlowe is a private detective working in downtown Los Angeles. A good-looking tough guy with a sharp tongue, he is well able to look after himself in his encounters with the underworld on the "mean streets" of LA. In *The Big Sleep*, Marlowe is hired to discover who is blackmailing the wayward daughter of an ailing millionaire general. Very soon he finds himself up to his neck in intrigue, double-crossing, false trails and dead bodies. Throughout all this he is never intimidated and always remains one step ahead of an occasionally corrupt police force. Sometimes tempted by the various beautiful women that cross his path, he constantly remains true to himself and his own code of honesty.

66 The blond flicked a short-barrelled gun out and stood pointing it at me. The pug sidled over flatfooted and felt my pockets with care. I turned around for him like a bored beauty modelling an evening gown. **99**

crime

Raymond Chandler was one of the most brilliant of crime novelists – witty, expert in creating atmosphere and always sympathetic to the under-dog. Written in 1939, *The Big Sleep* set the pattern for innumerable imitations featuring a fearless private detective operating in a shabby office who still manages to emerge with more dignity than all the rich, corrupt clients that come his way. Though it's sometimes difficult to keep up with all the plot details, Chandler's combination of suspenseful, pacey narrative and snappy dialogue has rarely been bettered. There are five other Philip Marlowe novels, of which the most memorable are *Farewell, My Lovely* and *The Long Goodbye*. All have been made into excellent films.

Recommended age: 13+

Gillian Cross
Calling a Dead Man
Oxford

An urn of ashes: that's all the family are left with when John Cox is killed in an explosion that goes badly wrong somewhere in Siberia. At least that's what the authorities say, claiming that they've identified him by his dental records. But John's sister Hayley is not convinced. She's watched him often and knows that John is a perfectionist, far too careful to have made any kind of mistake – especially an elementary one. So when John's fiancée Annie offers to accompany Hayley on a trip to Russia, she readily agrees. After all, perhaps seeing the site will answer some of questions that are bothering her.

crime

But once in Russia, Hayley and Annie find that there are still more questions than answers, and it's perfectly clear that there are a great many people who don't want them to be there. Despite endless attempts to throw them off the scent, and the dangers and difficulties that are put in their way, Hayley and Annie are determined to follow every lead in their search for the truth. Braving the bitter winter, they find the one thing that can link them to John and which gives them hope that he is still alive. This chilling thriller of intrigue and counter-intrigue depicts a place where Mafia power rules but the courage of individuals remains steadfast.

Recommended age: 11+

Arthur Conan Doyle
The Adventures of Sherlock Holmes
Oxford

Sherlock Holmes's powers of detection are so remarkable that he is able to work out intimate details about the lives of people he has never met before simply by observing them at close range. Holmes, who lives in lodgings in Baker Street, London, is assisted in his detective work by his devoted friend Dr Watson – the narrator of the adventures that they have together.

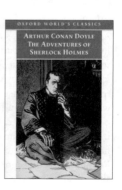

crime

Holmes's quick-wittedness – he is also a master of disguise – regularly astounds Dr Watson who (along with the regular police) is always rather slow to understand what is really going on. But Watson is brave and resourceful, and a rather easier character than his moody, highly-strung friend who passes the time between cases by playing the violin and taking cocaine.

> **66** ...as I looked up, I saw his tall, spare figure pass twice in a dark silhouette against the blind. He was pacing the room swiftly, eagerly, with his head sunk upon his chest and his hands clasped behind him. To me, who knew his every mood and habit, his attitude and manner told their own story. He was at work again. **99**

First published in the *Strand Magazine* at the end of the nineteenth century, these stories quickly became famous throughout the world. Set in a Victorian London of hansom cabs, gas lamps and steam trains, and peopled by over-sized villains, each story contains elaborate plot twists that regularly fool Watson – and most readers too – until Holmes finally puts everything right with an ingenious solution based on the most scrupulous logic. Conan Doyle also wrote full-length novels about Holmes and Watson, of which *The Hound of the Baskervilles* and *A Study in Scarlet* are the best.

Recommended age: 11+

crime

Anne Fine
The Tulip Touch
Puffin

No one likes Tulip. She hardly ever turns up for school, and when she does she only causes trouble. But Natalie, a new girl and the narrator of this story, succeeds in making friends with her before eventually wishing that she had never bothered. At first Tulip is good fun, but after a while the games she insists on playing begin taking a sinister turn. There are nasty practical jokes on other children, petty vandalism and some minor cruelty to animals. But when Tulip begins starting fires Natalie finally decides she has had enough. Her parents encourage the friendship because they feel sorry for Tulip who lives alone with her brutal father. Only Natalie knows quite how dangerous her best friend – and now her worst enemy – can be.

Unlike Tulip, Natalie comes from a stable family, although her parents tend to take their daughter for granted. Natalie can't help feeling sorry for Tulip, and still feels guilty even when her former friend has done her worst. For she knows how wretched her home life is, and how little anyone has ever done to try to make things better. In such circumstances, perhaps any

crime

child might turn out as bad. Written at a time when there was much debate in the press over whether some children could actually be born evil, *The Tulip Touch* shows how one child is poisoned not by her own nature but by the cruelty and neglect she suffers at home.

Recommended age: 11+

Ian Fleming
Casino Royale
Penguin

Commander James Bond, known to his employers in the British Secret Service as Agent 007, has a tough assignment. His villainous opposite number Le Chiffre, who works for the Russian spying unit SMERSH, is out to make money for his masters by gambling on the roulette tables in the south of France. Bond decides to take him on, and ends up winning a thrilling game of baccarat played for enormous stakes. Out for revenge, Le Chiffre captures Bond and sets about torturing him to death. But as always he manages to escape just in time, and with the help of the beautiful Vesper Lynd, a fast car, numerous gadgets and a number of violent deaths order is restored, at least until the next adventure. And there is still one last surprise to come, with Vesper Lynd revealed as not quite what she appeared.

This was the first of many James Bond stories. All the ingredients for future success are already in place, such as Bond's incredible technical skills in whatever

crime

situation he finds himself, his knowledge of wine, his super-human toughness and of course his effortless success with beautiful women. Brave, dedicated and with his own rough, but usually fair, sense of morality, he made an attractive figure for a country whose own place in the world was becoming ever more diminished when the book was written in 1955. Critics have disliked the snobbery in the Bond books, the fascination with violence and the old-fashioned attitude to women, who seem to exist primarily for the service of men. But the author knew how to tell a good story, and while some of the subsequent films became more and more unbelievable the books themselves are still recommendable for a truly exciting read.

Recommended age: 13+

Graham Greene
Brighton Rock
Vintage

Hale is an ex-crook trying to go straight; his enemies are his former gang headed by 17-year-old Pinkie, already a ruthless gangster. Hale quickly meets his death, but a day-tripper whom he met on Palace Pier becomes suspicious and Pinkie is forced to concoct an elaborate alibi. He does this by pretending to fall in love with the impressionable Rose, a waitress who is even younger than himself. But Pinkie starts to lose control, getting beaten up by hit-men from a bigger gang while his own group dwindles away. His only hope is to marry the still innocent Rose in order to stop any

crime

possibility of her becoming a witness against him in the future.

First published in 1938, this story can be read as a straight crime thriller, painting an unforgettable picture of the seedy side of Brighton and some of its more dubious inhabitants. But at another level, this is a novel that explores why it is that someone like Pinkie gives himself up to utter evil. Was it his childhood, where "hell lay about him in his infancy"? Could Pinkie have been saved by his former religious faith that he still can't quite shake off? The author himself, a Roman Catholic, often seems to be arguing with himself in this story about the nature of his faith and the way it could still be relevant to a lost soul like Pinkie. But at another level, he simply tells a brilliant story where double-crossing is the norm and razor-slashing the preferred way of settling differences between enemies.

Recommended age: 15+

John Grisham
The Firm
Arrow

Mitchell Y. McDeere, always known as Mitch, is young, poor and very, very clever. He's about to graduate from

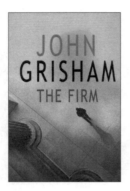

law school as one of the top lawyers in his year and he is after a good job. So when an unknown law firm in Memphis offers him a contract with a salary bigger than he could ever have dreamed of – with a brand-new BMW and low-interest mortgage thrown in – he cannot resist. Mitch and his young wife Abby move to Memphis and begin their new lives as employees of Bendini, Lambert and Locke, a conventional firm of tax lawyers.

Mitch knows he'll have to work hard, and he's determined to do so, but he soon discovers that the Firm wants his whole life, and it is ruthless about getting it. Through phone and wiretaps his employers know his every move and will stop at nothing, including blackmail, to get him to do what they want. They need Mitch and he needs to discover why. When he does work out just what it is that the Firm deals in, he has to move fast. Working with the FBI in a dizzying sequence of cross and double-cross against a background that crackles with danger, Mitch outsmarts his employers and finds freedom while bringing them to justice. John Grisham's ability to ratchet up the tension makes *The Firm* a genuinely scary thriller.

Recommended age: 15+

crime

David Guterson
Snow Falling on Cedars
Bloomsbury

The trial that lies at the heart of *Snow Falling on Cedars* makes a dramatic centrepiece to a multi-layered story of love and loss. Set in the small island community of San Piedro in the Pacific Northwest of America, it is a novel with a powerful sense of place and of the local community. When Carl Heine, a local fisherman, is found drowned, Kabuo Miyamoto is the first suspect in the murder enquiry. After all, the death blow looks as if it could have been delivered by "a Jap with a bloody gun butt" – and Kabuo is a young Japanese who could easily have delivered it. And there is a motive: Kabuo's family lost their land to Carl's during World War II. The background to the trial is the story of long-held prejudices against the Japanese, despite the fact that most, like Kabuo's family, have been settled for two generations. The American Japanese feel that they were badly treated by the US because they were held in internment; the Americans find them hard to forgive completely, as many fought the Japanese and still carry the scars.

crime

> **The accused man, Kabuo Miyamoto, sat proudly upright with a rigid grace, his palms placed softly on the defendant's table – the posture of a man who has detached himself insofar as this is possible at his own trial.** ""

As the different characters from the island community gather in the courtroom and play their parts in the trial, the long-standing friendships, loves and losses of Kabuo and Carl, Kabuo's wife Hatsue and, above all, Ishmael Chambers, the local newspaper reporter, begin to unfold in a story which is both satisfyingly tense and romantic.

Recommended age: 15+

Robert Harris
Fatherland
Arrow

Fatherland is a gripping political thriller in which Robert Harris rewrites history. Centred on a murder mystery, the story explores the sinister possibilities of what things might have been like if Hitler had won World War II.

It's April 1964. The new Berlin created by Hitler's architect Albert Speer is now the centre of the powerful Third Reich, an empire stretching from the Rhine to the Urals, and plans are underway for celebrating Hitler's 75th birthday. Xavier March, a homicide investigator with the Berlin Kriminalpolizei – known as the "Krippo" – is detailed to investigate the case of a body found floating in Lake Havel. When the body is identified as that of Buhler, a former high-ranking officer serving mostly in the east of the empire, March asks why. Working alone, and increasingly against the authorities, March follows a trail that delves deep into the past, into the heart of the Nazi regime, uncovering corruption at all levels, from Swiss bank accounts to the darkest secrets of the extermination of the Jews. Though once a member of the SS, and with a son who is still committed to the Nazi cause, March is now a critic of the mighty German government. What he discovers fills him with horror and puts his life in great danger.

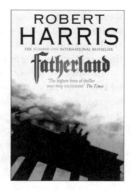

Recommended age: 15+

S.E. Hinton
The Outsiders
Puffin

The nights are hot and the boys are bored. Greasers and Socs, two gangs from the opposite sides of town, are out cruising the streets. They're looking for action, but action can all too easily turn to trouble whenever the two gangs meet. Out in their convertibles, the wealthy Socs sneer at the posturing Greasers, who, with their

crime

trademark long and slicked hair, stake out their own territory in the town. No one wants all-out warfare, but a small incident sparks a fight and frighteningly soon things get completely out of control.

The story is told in as matter-of-fact a way as possible by Ponyboy, the youngest of three brothers struggling to keep together after the death of their parents. Playing down the horror, he highlights the true feelings of those involved – kids who would be seen as "trouble" by most adults. Their story is one of yearning and loss: of insecurity and a search for identity.

S.E. Hinton wrote *The Outsiders* while she was still at high school, which gives her the advantage of being able to level with her characters. The book captures the authentic details of adolescent speech and emotion; even more than that, it conveys all the confusion and chaos that make that period of life so difficult and unpredictable.

Recommended age: 13+

P.D. James
Shroud for a Nightingale
Faber

Nightingale House, a Victorian edifice with four turrets standing proudly in each corner, is an imposing place, but not suitable for training nurses – so thinks Miss Beale, the visiting inspector, as she draws up at its doors. Her worst fears are confirmed when a student acting as a patient in a demonstration is brutally murdered. Though Nurse Pearce was never one of the most popular nurses, no one would have wanted her killed, but the death was so immediate that someone in their small and sheltered community must have done it. The local CID is called and an investigation gets underway. Almost before it's begun, however, another nurse is found dead, also poisoned. Who is the killer in their midst? Inspector Adam Dalgleish is brought in to get to the bottom of the mystery.

66 She stood absolutely still for a moment looking down at Fallon's body, and smiling a little as if surprised. She had no doubt that Fallon was dead. The eyes were still wide open but they were cold and opaque, like the eyes of a dead fish. 99

The tight-knit community of nurses provides an interesting and varied cast, and P.D. James makes sure that each has a distinct personality as their foibles,

crime

desires, aspirations and lies are laid bare under Dalgleish's careful questioning. It's a subtle technique, one which explores the vagaries of human nature and what motivates individual and collective action. As ever, James lays many false trails, leaving the reader guessing until the very end.

Recommended age: 15+

Anthony Masters
Wicked
Orchard

Though inevitably always a bit of an outsider, Josh gets on well with his older twin brothers. Usually they let him join in – though he's not quite up to their level, especially at sport. But everything changes one summer holiday when the boys are left alone while Mum and Dad run a summer school. The days seems hard to fill, especially when Josh realizes that Jack and Tom have a secret. They change towards him and even towards each other. A fight turns nasty – not the usual kind of play-fighting between the twins – and when Josh overhears Tom say, "We've got to tell someone. We can't leave him there," he knows they're hiding something. As the long, hot days of the summer holidays slowly roll past, Josh realizes that whatever it is his brothers are keeping secret, it has changed them – and him – for ever.

Set in a busy family where both parents are occupied with their own business, *Wicked* is observed through Josh's eyes; he is on the threshold of adolescence, sometimes longing for the old certainties of his

crime

childhood, sometimes keen to be included in the exploits of the older boys. Menacing and dark, *Wicked* is a terrific thriller that crackles with tension from the very first moment.

Recommended age: 11+

Philip Pullman
The Tiger in the Well
Scholastic

Sally Lockhart is already a controversial enough figure as an unmarried mother working as a detective in late Victorian Britain. But things become even more difficult for her when a man to whom she has never been married suddenly sues her for divorce. Threatened with the loss of her 2-year-old daughter, she is forced into hiding, relying on the help of her friends. She also gets to know Daniel Goldberg, the brilliant left-wing leader of London's new immigrant Jewish population who is, in turn, threatened by agitators at the command of the sinister figure behind all of Sally's trouble.

66 Sally shook her head as Big Ben struck three, and set out across the bridge at a smart pace. On the south bank she turned right towards Lambeth, and for the next two hours she just walked hard. She didn't know that side of the river and before long she was lost. 99

crime

Better known for his fantasy novels, Philip Pullman is also a successful writer of thrillers that are set in

Victorian London but which carry modern political overtones. Always on the side of the poor and dispossessed, he shows how hard it was for anyone to survive on the unfashionable margins of a prosperous society. Even Sally herself has to make a journey of understanding when she finally realizes that her own previously comfortable circumstances had relied on the exploitation of others unable to protect themselves. The descriptions of the additional problems facing immigrants escaping from cruelty and oppression abroad, but now at the mercy of criminals in Britain, are moving and often uncomfortable, given their modern parallels. The final, explosive climax, which brings together all the characters met so far, is unlikely ever to be forgotten. For more about Sally and her friends, try *The Ruby in the Smoke* and *The Shadow in the North*.

Recommended age: 11+

Bali Rai
The Crew
Corgi

Five British teenagers, three male and two female, from different racial backgrounds make up an unofficial gang – 'the crew'. Each member depends heavily on the others, which is just as well given that they are all growing up in an often dangerous urban ghetto where drug dealers and prostitutes are everyday sights. Things go wrong when one of them finds a hidden bag

crime

containing £15,000. Handing this in to the police does not mean the end of their troubles, which lead to kidnapping, violence and finally murder. But by involving their parents and their partners, some sort of order is finally restored. And by now there is love interest as well, with four members of the crew becoming romantically involved with each other.

Gang stories, with their strong sense of loyalty and inclusion, have long been popular, but this one breaks many of the unofficial rules found in this type of fiction. Far from thinking they can always manage on their own, the crew know that they need adult help to get them out of their difficulties. The villains they are up against are not easily outwitted; instead, they come across as vicious and ruthless, not to be messed with by ambitious adolescents playing at detectives. But far from painting an unrelentingly depressing picture, Bali Rai takes a positive view of the ghetto and its young occupants. Their courage, humour and resourcefulness remain constant whatever else is happening to them.

Recommended age: 13+

crime

Dorothy L. Sayers
The Nine Tailors

New English Library

When Lord Peter Wimsey gets his Daimler stuck in a ditch on his way through Fenchurch St Paul on a grey day at the end of December, he finds himself having to stay in the local rectory while it's repaired. The rector is very proud of his church and particularly of the famous bells – the Nine Tailors. Lord Peter happens to be an expert bell-ringer, so, when one of the local team is taken ill, he steps in to ring out the complicated nine-hour peal with which the village traditionally celebrates the coming of the New Year. It marks the beginning of Lord Peter's involvement with the Nine Tailors, some of which are rung again only a few days later when Lady Thorpe dies. Her death leads Lord Peter to hear the complicated story of a robbery which, despite the arrest of two local men, remains partly unsolved. A few months later, Lord Peter is invited back to Fenchurch St Paul when a battered body is found.

Against a background of bells and bell-ringing, Lord Peter sets out to solve both the burglary and the murder which haunt the village. With a large cast of convincing village characters and a plot that twists and turns, *The Nine Tailors* is a rewardingly complicated story, and one of the very best of Sayers's novels involving the suave amateur detective Lord Peter Wimsey.

Recommended age: 13+

crime

Irvine Welsh

Trainspotting

Vintage

Through a series of interconnected stories, *Trainspotting* gives a grimly honest picture of the life of people living at the bottom of Edinburgh society. Written in dialect and told entirely from within the community – without judgement or criticism – it describes the different characters' existence in a drug-ridden culture dominated by addiction, attempts to break out of addiction and the depressing return to it.

Renton, Sick Boy, Spud and the Begbie are nihilistic and cynical about the society they live in. For them, the horizon stretches only as far as begging, stealing, abusing any and every system possible, and shooting up. They are partly out of control, and partly highly controlling, in that they keep just the right side of staying alive: for them the highs from heroin are irresistible and they are prisoners of it. The only glimmer of hope lies in Renton's desire to get clean.

Trainspotting is at times hopeless and depressing, but there are moments of optimism and an infusion of

crime

manic, if sometimes desperate, humour. The book became a cult novel when it was published in 1993 (and filmed in 1996), not least because it pictured the lives of many who had previously been ignored – a picture both terrifying and intoxicating.

Recommended age: 15+

Chris Wooding
Kerosene
Scholastic

Cal loves fire. It makes him feel confident and helps him to cope. And Cal needs a lot of help – shy, uneasy around others, he's a loner, though fine with his best mate Joel when there's no one else around. At school, he pours his energies into his art, and tries to keep to the sidelines. But when Emma and Abby set out to wind him up by pretending to fancy him, Cal gets seriously confused – and the fires get seriously out-of-hand. First there's the hay barn, then the disused factory. Finally, Cal has one last fire, a fire to end it all – and through it finds a surprising way out.

Chris Wooding was only 21 when he wrote *Kerosene* and its realism is convincing. Everything rings true: Cal and Joel and their lifestyle, their continual run-ins with teachers and authority, their experiences around clubs, smoking dope and drinking too much. Above all, Cal's search for an identity and his driving need for a sense of himself carry total conviction.

Recommended age: 13+

crime

adventure

Isabel Allende
City of the Beasts
Flamingo

Fifteen-year-old Alexander's
normal, cheerful life in
California is interrupted
when his mother becomes
seriously ill. Sent to live with
his reporter-grandmother, he
finds himself accompanying
her on an expedition to the
Amazon rainforest in order
to track down a legendary
creature known as 'the Beast'.
But some of those on the trip
have other ideas, including
the poisoning of the People

of the Mist – one of the last headhunting tribes – in
order to steal their land. With the help of Nadia,
daughter of the local guide, Alexander finds a way of
warning these people before the worst can happen. He
also encounters the Beast itself.

> 'These vials do not contain vaccines but
> deadly doses of the measles virus.' Captain
> Ariosto's response was to aim his pistol and
> shoot Karakawe in the chest.

This story has been described as an ecological
thriller, and there is no doubt that the author is on the

side of those threatened with extinction. As she clearly shows, the real enemy is not some fabled Beast but the greed and coarseness of modern civilization itself. But although she is keen to show readers something of the dignity and wisdom found in indigenous tribes, this is still first and foremost a story – well written, sharply characterized and never predictable. To read it is like visiting the Amazon rainforest itself, the astonishing beauty of which is now threatened as never before. Two more stories are planned in this series; if they are as good as this one they should be well worth looking out for when the time comes.

Recommended age: 11+

Beryl Bainbridge
The Birthday Boys

Penguin

Fact and fiction are cleverly woven together in Beryl Bainbridge's hugely readable version of Captain Scott's fateful expedition to the South Pole. Told in short chapters through the eyes of five non-survivors, it charts the years of the expedition, providing a great adventure story as well as giving an on-the-spot feel of the hardships, the chaos and the motivation

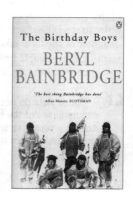

adventure

of everyone who took part. Fraught with tragedy –
handled in a deliberately detached way – it is a deeply
emotional book.

In Bainbridge's version, the myth of Scott as a great
leader and his team as men of outstanding courage is
replaced by an account of leadership tempered by
stubbornness and ill-planning, and of bravery by
stupidity. She looks behind the romantic image of
Scott as a great British hero and describes an arrogant
and foolish man who rashly led his team to their
death. But this is far more than just an account of a
real expedition, it is also a beautifully and sparely
written story about why the different individuals took
part and how they interacted in the frozen wastes of
the Antarctic. It's a book of insight and honesty set
against a background in which the gruelling conditions
of the cold are all too tangible.

Recommended age: 13+

Pat Barker
Regeneration
Penguin

The struggle for sanity is the underlying thread of
Regeneration. Set in Craiglockhart, an imposing
psychiatric hospital on the outskirts of Edinburgh, it
tells the story of Dr Rivers and the shell-shocked young
soldiers sent to him for treatment during World War I.
Physically and mentally scarred, the inmates of
Craiglockhart are further traumatized by the deliberate

adventure

misrepresentation of the conflict, which means that the general public – and their relatives – has no idea of the reality of the trenches. Rivers's patients include Siegfried Sassoon, a distinguished poet and an officer, who has been referred to Craiglockhart because of the anti-war material he has been writing.

Though based on the true stories of Sassoon and Rivers, *Regeneration* is also a superb work of fiction. Pat Barker gives a harrowing and honest insight into the deep and sometimes irreparable damage that World War I did to those who took part in it. She is as unflinching in her descriptions of the war itself as in her depiction of those harmed by it – and by the terrifying nature of their treatment. But Barker also goes beyond the detail of the war and gives a fine view of the rigid and narrow-minded class system of the period. *Regeneration*, the first in a trilogy, is followed by *The Eye in the Door* and *The Ghost Road*.

Recommended age: 15+

C.S. Forester
The Hornblower Novels
Penguin

Horatio Hornblower is only 17 when he joins his first ship. Despite his unfortunate reputation as the midshipman who was seasick even before putting out to sea, Hornblower is never demoralized by the mockery he encounters. He rapidly becomes an outstanding young officer who unfailingly performs and often exceeds his duties while always doing his best for the men under his command. The navy at the time of the Napoleonic wars was a sickeningly brutal service, and needed officers of Horatio's calibre to set a good example. Hornblower is as decent a fictional hero as it is possible to find, even though he has his faults – such as a tendency to think he always knows best. But in battle there is no one braver, and if ever an adventure suggests itself, Horatio will be the first to volunteer. He has enemies within the service, however, and some of his best exploits show him fighting not just the French but also some of the rotten apples within the navy itself.

Although the Hornblower novels lack the psychological depth of Patrick O'Brian's Aubrey-Maturin books, they bring the period of the Napoleonic wars and their aftermath vividly to life. Plainly and effectively written, there are eleven titles in total, covering Hornblower's career from lowly midshipman to prestigious admiral. Ten of them are contained in three omnibus editions – *The Young Hornblower Omnibus*, *Captain Hornblower RN* and *Admiral Hornblower*.

Recommended age: 11+

George MacDonald Fraser
The Flashman Papers
HarperCollins

Harry Flashman is an absolute bounder, a genuine rotter. After he was deservedly expelled from Rugby School in the late 1830s, he joins the army as a base for becoming an adventurer overseas. Never afraid to lie and always after the main chance, he later surfaces in Afghanistan, China, the United States, Russia and many other places whenever there is a bit of action that he might profit from. Dark, with heavy sideburns and a flamboyant moustache, and fatally attractive to the opposite sex, Harry behaves as badly with them as he does with everyone else. An expert duellist, he is normally able to escape from danger just in time, and when he can't there is always the chance of tricking himself out of trouble. He is not the kind of man that any decent person would wish to know.

Harry is an imaginary character who first surfaces as the school bully in Thomas Hughes' famous Victorian novel *Tom Brown's Schooldays*. George MacDonald Fraser had the idea of writing further adventures around this character once he became an adult. Each story takes place at some important historical moment, such as the Peking riots or the American War of Independence, and is narrated as if part of the memoirs of the elderly Brigadier General Flashman. As well as enjoying the wit and general exuberance of these tales, readers can learn some history, too, since the author is always meticulous in getting his facts right. So far, Fraser has completed eleven Flashman novels (known collectively as *The*

Flashman Papers) from *Flashman* in 1969 to *Flashman and the Tiger* in 1999.

Recommended age: 13+

Esther Freud
Hideous Kinky
Penguin

'Hideous' and 'kinky', two apparently unlinked and meaningless words, become a mantra for Maretta and Bea. Chanted to each other, they become a secure fixed point for the girls as they travel on an uncertain and unpredictable journey through Morocco, dragged along by a mother who is in search of perfect bliss and spiritual fulfilment.

Maretta is 5 and longs to go home; her bossy older sister insists on going to school. Everything is seen from Maretta's viewpoint. She gives a vivid impression of the sights, smells and atmosphere of Morocco, with all its heat, colour and dust. Despite her age, her impressions are far from superficial; she observes accurately but without excessive judgement. She accepts Moroccan peasants and the eccentric Europeans she encounters with equal composure, taking them all in her stride as she experiences the swings between elation and despair that often go with long-distance travel. Unlike most travellers, she has nothing to prove, so there is no bravado in this story, only a charming acceptance of everything she witnesses.

Based on Esther Freud's own childhood, *Hideous Kinky* is in part a glorious and celebratory travel

adventure

adventure – but its originality lies in her exceptional instinct for the ways in which children view the adult world.

Recommended age: 15+

Cornelia Funke
The Thief Lord
Chicken House

Two orphaned children, Bo and Prosper, are on the run in Venice. They are escaping from the cruel uncle and aunt who want to adopt the younger one while sending the other away to a boarding school. With their money running out, the children join a gang of children living rough in an old, disused cinema. They are all sustained by Scipio, also known as the Thief Lord, a boy who lives apart from the others and always comes up with stolen money and goods when they are most needed. All the valuables the children steal are sold to Barbarossa, an evil, red-bearded shop-owner who also acts as a fence. But when Victor, a gentle private detective with a love of tortoises, gets on the case, Bo and Prosper face discovery and the end of their independence.

The reality of children running away from home and living rough is far from romantic. But this story is more a magical-mystery tour than anything else, playing up the fun side of living without parents and never becoming too seriously involved with the real underworld of burglary and other petty crime. It should be read as an exciting, modern fairy tale, set in one of the most beautiful cities in the world. Translated from the original German, this quirky, unpredictable and constantly good-humoured story is always a pleasure to read.

Recommended age: 11+

Alex Garland
The Beach
Penguin

Newly arrived in Bangkok, Richard heads straight for the Khao San Road, heart of backpacker life, where almost every house is a cheap guesthouse and where, like Richard, almost every traveller pauses before heading off elsewhere into Thailand. But on his first night, a fellow traveller slits his wrists, leaving Richard his map. The map is of 'The Beach' – a secret, idyllic lagoon, cut off from the rest of the world by the jungle but with its own freshwater supply. Here, so it is rumoured, perfection can be found. Teaming up with Etienne and Françoise, a French couple, Richard sets off to find this nirvana. But what is this community, and is it as idyllic as it sounds? He uncovers more than he'd

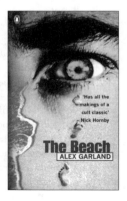

'Has all the makings of a cult classic'
– Nick Hornby

The Beach
ALEX GARLAND

adventure

bargained for in this gripping adventure story, which remains full of surprises until the very end.

Alex Garland tells the story through Richard's eyes, writing directly and vividly to capture not only the place, which provides a dazzling background of palm trees, hot sand and brilliant blue sea, but also the individual members of the community, who are sharply drawn and entirely credible as they play their roles in the final tragedy.

Recommended age: 15+

Alan Garner
Red Shift
Collins

Three stories separated in time but each linked to the other make up this challenging but always gripping book. All centre on an old church and former sacred spot in the north of England. The first is set at the end of the Roman occupation, the second at the time of the Civil War during the seventeenth century, while the third concerns a modern teenage couple. All contain conflict that is sometimes both savage and raw, in two cases ending in a sickening massacre. The modern

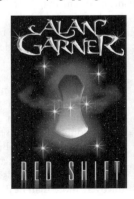

couple, Tom and Jan, while deeply in love, reach a crisis in their relationship due to the opposition of parents and Jan's involvement with another man. The couples in the previous two stories also go through similar difficulties, and Tom himself finally becomes aware of these other characters who lived so long before him.

> **He was holding a smooth shape. It was polished, grey green, and looked like an axe head made of stone.**

Alan Garner is not an easy writer, and much of *Red Shift* is told in dialogue that sometimes leaves the reader with the job of making out what is actually happening. True to form, Garner ends his book with two pages written in code which readers must work out for themselves. But for those who stick with this story there are many rewards. The author has always been fascinated by the way that history intrudes into the present; he also believes that humans are bound to repeat certain patterns of actions found in the past. Most importantly of all, he writes so well and with such conviction that the story itself always gets through.

Recommended age: 13+

Mark Haddon
The Curious Incident of the Dog in the Night-time
Jonathan Cape

Although Christopher Boone is unlike any other adventure hero, his story turns out to be genuinely

adventure

heroic. For Christopher has Asperger's syndrome, a form of autism, which in his case takes the form of an amazing facility for maths, an intense fear of crowds, obsessional behaviour (he can't bear the colours yellow and brown), an aversion to being touched and an inability to understand jokes or tell a lie. Living with his flawed but basically loving father, Christopher is prompted to run away to London. But how will he cope, never having travelled on his own before?

This extraordinary book is written as if told by Christopher himself, and the narrative jumps from odd bits of general knowledge to typically over-exact answers to the various questions put to him. Though not easy to live with, Christopher still comes across as someone who does his best against difficult odds. Although people close to him are supportive, those not used to his oddness are often less sympathetic – making Christopher's epic journey from Swindon to London a severe trial for all concerned. How he survives is exciting, moving, occasionally comic, and always highly involving.

Recommended age: 13+

adventure

Karen Hesse
Young Nick's Head
Simon & Schuster

Nick Young's diary describes three thrilling years at sea; three years that take him on Captain Cook's historic voyage to Australia aboard the *Endeavour*. Eleven-year-old Nick is a butcher's apprentice who runs away from his cruel master and uncaring father. Desperate, he stows away on the first boat he finds in Plymouth harbour, where he manages to remain hidden for some time before starvation gets the better of him. Once out in the open, Nick becomes part of the eighty-man crew as they work their way across the world towards an unknown country.

Each entry is brief, but through them Nick gives a clear picture of the different members of the crew – including Captain Cook, whose skill, courage and vision inspire the trip – as well as the exciting new places they see and the often terrifying conditions. Life at sea is hard, but Nick soon makes friends on board, especially with the ship's surgeon Dr Monkhouse and Mr Banks the botanist, who do their best to protect him from the worst brutalities of his shipmates and the ever-present dangers of fever and starvation. Karen Hesse skilfully conveys the hardship and excitement of life on board ship, combining immediacy with historical accuracy.

Recommended age: 11+

adventure

Homer
The Odyssey
Penguin

The Odyssey tells the story of how Odysseus makes his long and eventful journey home to Ithaca after the Trojan War. But it is also a tale of the loyalty of his wife Penelope, who has to resist the many suitors who wish to step into Odysseus's shoes, and of his son Telemachus. Originally an oral poem written down in Greek nearly three thousand years ago, the *Odyssey* is an ancient 'epic' – a tale of heroism and mythology, vast in scope yet overflowing with rich narrative detail. Odysseus has all the attributes of a hero – such as strength and courage – but he also employs cunning in his various escapades, and is sufficiently flawed to be believably human.

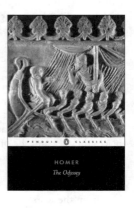

The story begins while Odysseus is still away, detained by the nymph Calypso who longs to marry him. Eventually the gods conspire to help and so the hero is released to begin his journey home. Once under way, he is wrecked in a violent storm raised by the sea god Poseidon, but lands safely on the shores of the Phaeacians. Here he tells of his amazing adventures during ten years of wandering: the land of the Lotus Eaters, where all of his men who ate from the lotus were crazed by its narcotic power; his meeting with the Cyclops, whose hideous single eye he puts out with a stake; Circe, who turned his men into pigs; the Sirens whose songs lure men to their death, and whom he only avoided by making his men tie him to the mast; and the twin trap of the six-headed monster Scylla, who had to be appeased if Odysseus was to avoid the violent whirlpool, Charybdis. It's spell-binding stuff: each is a wonderful story of invention and trickery in which gods and humans take part.

There are many English versions of the *Odyssey*, all very different in style. The prose translation by E.V. Rieu was the first ever Penguin Classic (it has recently been updated by his son D.C.H. Rieu), but readers after a vivid verse translation might be tempted by Robert Fagles's newer version, also in Penguin.

Recommended age: 13+

Anthony Horowitz
Stormbreaker
Walker

A latter-day, under-age James Bond, 14-year-old Alex Rider is thrust into the action when his uncle Ian, who is also his guardian, dies in a tragic car crash. From then on, everything that Alex has known is changed. Forced into becoming the youngest-ever agent for MI6, Alex undergoes tough training before being sent off on

adventure

his first mission – armed with suitable hardware, of course.

Stormbreaker is all high drama and often ridiculous, but Horowitz skilfully makes Alex an almost convincing teenager, even though he's operating in a world of high-octane derring-do. Alex sees himself through some hair-raising adventures, escaping through good judgement and a lot of luck. A spy story thriller with enough tongue-in-cheek to show that it's not taking itself too seriously, *Stormbreaker* has all the excitement and drama you'd expect from the genre. Alex's adventures continue in *Point Blanc* and *Skeleton Key*.

Recommended age: 11+

Richard Hughes
A High Wind in Jamaica
Vintage

Set in the nineteenth century, *A High Wind in Jamaica* tells of how seven British schoolchildren, travelling from the West Indies to England, are kidnapped by pirates. When it becomes impossible to return them to their original boat, children and pirates are thrown together for a long voyage. Unexpectedly, they get on well; with the children not missing their parents in the least as they play with the ship's monkey, climb the rigging and generally enjoy themselves. The good-humoured pirates put up with them patiently until a disastrous second raid leads to Emily, one of the children, stabbing to death a captured, tied-up sea captain whom she thinks is trying to attack her. When the Royal Navy eventually catches the boat, it is the pirates who get the blame for this, with Emily treated as a heroine.

> 66 The children's only enemy on board the schooner (which presently put to sea again, with them on board) was the big white pig. 99

Like *Lord of the Flies*, this is a novel that takes a completely unsentimental look at children. They are shown as self-centred, forgetful of those they loved, far more concerned about animals than with their fellow humans and living only for the moment. The pirates themselves come over as much softer targets, unselfishly looking after the children and quite unprepared for the final betrayal where Emily says enough to get them all hanged. As the author puts it, too late did 'those unfortunate men at last realize what diabolical yeast had been introduced to their lump'.

Recommended age: 13+

Geraldine McCaughrean
The Kite Rider

Oxford

Set in thirteenth-century China, *The Kite Rider* tells of the adventures of Gou Haoyou, whose life is turned upside-down when he sees his father killed in an accident after being tricked into becoming a human wind-tester. When his own mother looks set to marry

adventure

the very man who killed his father, Haoyou seems powerless to stop him.

But stop him he must, and Haoyou leaves the complex intrigues of his family, setting out on a long and dangerous journey that will both save his mother and bring him nearer to the spirit of his dead father. Haoyou joins the Jade Circus, a miscellaneous bunch of tricksters and charlatans, who travel the length and breadth of the country entertaining the gullible peasants before reaching their ultimate goal – the court of the great Kublai Khan. Strapped to a kite that sails up into the sky, Haoyou takes messages to and from the spirit world. His bird's-eye view also gives him a new perspective on people: he learns whom to trust, and sees into the secret schemes of those who look so respectable. He also sees behind the secrets of different communities and, above all, he discovers his own feelings about his parents and himself. Part-adventure, part-travelogue, *The Kite Rider* is a richly imagined and funny roller-coaster of near misses and lucky chances, which Haoyou rides with the nerve of any hero.

Recommended age: 11+

adventure

Patrick O'Brian
The Aubrey-Maturin Novels
HarperCollins

Jack Aubrey is a bluff, brave sailor who after many
reverses eventually becomes an admiral in the British
navy. Nearly all his professional life is spent in
skirmishes against the French fleet as part of the long
drawn out Napoleonic wars. His great friend, the ship's
doctor Stephen Maturin, is also a spy for the British –
something Jack knows enough about never to ask any
questions. They are very different characters, with Jack
hearty and open while Stephen is inward-looking and
scholarly. Surrounding these two characters are various
other seamen who always choose to sail with Jack since
he has the reputation of being lucky as well as good to
his men. In particular, he has an uncanny ability to spot
and capture rich enemy ships, so ensuring a generous
handout to his otherwise poorly paid crew.

Patrick O'Brian writes about every detail of naval life
at this time in history, and there are many close
descriptions of how battles are fought and storms
weathered. But this is also the story of two very distinct
individuals up against red tape and corruption at home
and enemy plotting abroad. Matters are further
complicated by Jack's inability to manage his own
finances when he is on land and Stephen's unhappy
relations with his beautiful but mostly absent wife.
There are twenty books in this sequence, with a
growing number of young and older fans happy to
follow this pair on their extraordinary adventures set

adventure

against the background of the brutal realities of late eighteenth-century naval life.

Recommended age: 13+

Celia Rees
Truth or Dare
Macmillan

Thirteen-year-old Josh and his mother have to spend the summer in the house of his grandmother, who is slowly dying. One day she talks about an Uncle Patrick who is said to have died at the age that Josh is now. Up in the attic, he finds his uncle's old trunk, full of strange possessions, including numbers of science fiction comics. Josh becomes convinced there is more to this story than he has been told. He gets his mother to admit that her brother Patrick suffered from a form of autism that cut him off from others, and in particular from his own, impatient father. His mother meanwhile is also writing a novel closely based on Patrick that Josh secretly reads. Finally he finds out about the tragic accident that led to Patrick being shut away for the rest of his life. He also discovers that his uncle is still alive.

The truth about what happened in the past is something that always has to be taken on trust by those who were not alive to witness it. But occasionally the past is distorted or even completely rewritten when it contains secrets that people want to conceal. Such is the case in this fine novel, which reads with all the excitement of a detective story as Josh gradually pieces together the clues he finds around him about his unworldly, deluded but still charming lost uncle who has been written out of family history. Despite its sad subject matter, and for all its shocks and surprises, this is finally a story about forgiveness and understanding.

Recommended age: 13+

Rosemary Sutcliff
The Eagle of the Ninth
Oxford

Marcus is determined to discover what happened to his father's legion, the Ninth, which went missing in mysterious circumstances near the great wall that divides the Roman empire from the marauding Picts in the north of Britain. Together with his newly freed slave, Esca, Marcus sets out on the journey north, unsure of what he'll find – if anything – but hopeful that something will remain. Marcus is driven by a desire to prove the heroism that the Roman empire stands for and to reclaim some honour for his dead father, but, by the time he finds the eagle – now a broken symbol, but still one that is worshipped – Marcus has learnt the value of the old ways, the ways of the Dark people with whom he finally chooses to live.

The Eagle of the Ninth is a story of great humanity, in which the declining Roman empire is shown in a domestic light. The invading Romans have become integrated, marrying with the indigenous Britons and

adventure

setting up homes and families. Alongside the
excitement and drama of Marcus's search lies the story
of his growing understanding of other people and their
ways. *The Silver Branch* and *The Lantern Bearers* follow
it in the series.

Recommended age: 11+

Mark Twain
The Adventures of Huckleberry Finn
Penguin

Huck, as everyone calls him, lives with Widow Douglas
and her sister Miss Watson in the American South
towards the end of the nineteenth century. But he is
still in danger from his worthless father, who eventually
kidnaps and imprisons his
son in an effort to trace
some lost money. Huck
escapes, but rather than go
back to respectability, he
sails away down the
Mississippi River on a raft
in the company of Jim, a
runaway slave. Despite
coming across murderers,
lynch mobs and feuding
clans on their journey, the
couple survives, finally
returning home to find that
Jim has already been

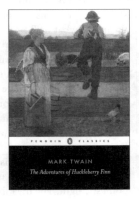

adventure

granted his freedom. Faced by the prospect of another well-meaning adult 'going to adopt me and sivilize me', Huck starts planning his next escape.

> **66** After breakfast I wanted to talk about the dead man and guess out how he come to be killed, but Jim didn't want to. He said it would fetch bad luck; and besides, he said, he might come back and ha'nt us… **99**

Told in dialect, as if by Huck himself, this story combines humour with an unflinching look at humans at their best and worst. Planned as a sequel to the same author's *The Adventures of Tom Sawyer,* it is a far more ambitious and moving story, with Huck and Jim witnessing a variety of strange goings-on down the river at a time when Americans were used to taking the law into their own hands. While the author was opposed to slavery, some of the words Huck and others use to describe Jim now seem very offensive. But Huck is good at heart, with a strong moral sense and an independent spirit. His story will find an echo with any reader who has dreamed of breaking away from routine in search of adventure.

Recommended age: 13+

adventure

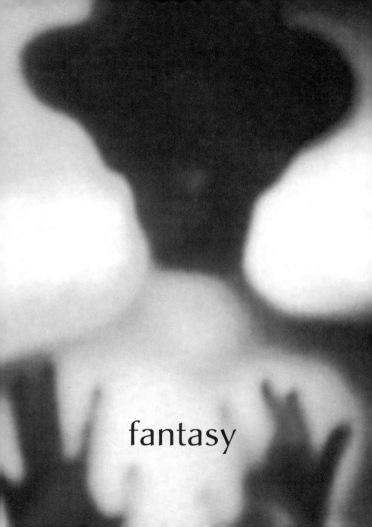

fantasy

David Almond
Skellig
Hodder

Michael is worried: worried
about his baby sister, whose
precarious health leads to
constant visits to hospital;
worried by the upheaval of
moving to a ramshackle
new house with dodgy
plumbing. He needs a few
certainties to make life
more bearable – and he
needs something to believe
in. In Skellig, a crumpled
figure mostly hidden
behind rubbish in the

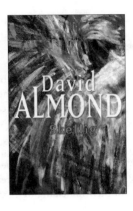

tumbled-down garage, he finds both. Part-human,
part-angel, Skellig is restored to health by Michael
with the help of a regular supply of Chinese
takeaways. Michael's parents have forbidden him
from entering the garage, and no one else knows
about the strange creature's presence except for
Michael's new friend Mina.

Skellig is a wonderfully seamless blend of reality and
magic. Michael believes in Skellig, but did he invent
him or is he real? He certainly provides a vital point of
security for Michael when the most important things in
his own life seem threatened, and it is through his
involvement with Skellig that Michael ultimately comes

fantasy

to feel more actively involved in the struggle for the survival of his baby sister.

Recommended age: 11+

Natalie Babbitt
Tuck Everlasting
Bloomsbury

Just one drink from the bubbling spring hidden deep in the forest has changed the Tuck family forever. They cannot grow older, they cannot die – in fact, they cannot change in any way at all. They have drunk from the spring of immortality. But this does not make life any easier for them. For a time they can stay in one place, but after a while people notice that they never grow older. They never reveal their secret or the source of their life-changing elixir until, by mistake, they are

spotted having a refreshing gulp. Determined to prevent young Winnie from imitating them and suffering the same fate, the Tucks kidnap her and explain their predicament.

Eloquently and lyrically written with enormous sympathy for the Tuck family's predicament, Natalie Babbitt's novel raises important and interesting questions about

fantasy

the value of life, the fear of dying, and the need to break away from families.

Recommended age: 13+

Herbie Brennan
Faerie Wars
Bloomsbury

The day starts badly for 14-year-old Henry when he discovers that his parents' marriage is on the rocks. The only real friend he can confide in is Mr Fogarty, an elderly and grumpy ex-bank robber with astounding technical skills. It is through him that Henry discovers Pyrgus, a boy his age who comes from a different world. Henry follows Pyrgus back to where he came from in order to help him. For everyone is out to get Pyrgus, from Silas Brimstone, a wicked factory owner, to Lord Hairstreak, the ruthless leader of the opposition to Pyrgus's king-father. Excitement reaches an unbearable pitch but Pyrgus survives, although not before some severe punishment and a couple of near disasters.

Fairies often have a bad name where older readers are concerned, but in this novel they are anything but sweet and pretty. The author writes about them as tough,

fantasy

capable creatures. In his own world, Pyrgus has to cope with recognizable human problems when it comes to his difficult relationship with his austere but noble father, also under constant threat from assorted villains and demons. And so the plot bubbles on in this sometimes violent but always entertaining book, written in a style so readable that the end – after 368 pages – still comes much too soon.

Recommended age: 11+

Hans Magnus Enzensberger
Where Were You, Robert?
Penguin

When Robert disappears, nobody notices as his journey is in his head. While his body stays quietly at home, Robert runs his own private film show. Of course, he's careful not to let anyone else see it happening but once it starts Robert can stare into a film or TV screen or painting, and find himself drawn into the time and space depicted. Travelling backwards in time, he can ride as a highwayman or take part in the tricks of sorcery. He's even able to meet his grandmother – when she was a little girl. Robert takes

fantasy

off through pictures and photographs, shifting from one time to another and always going further and further from his own home.

> **Of course no one knows what Robert sees before he goes to sleep. Robert is no fool. He takes good care not to let on about his own private film show. He knows exactly what his father would say if he heard about it. You're crazy, he'd say.**

It's a wonderfully original device for exploration as there are no limits to where Robert can travel and no problems of access. But just because the travelling is easy it doesn't mean that Robert isn't on a journey of discovery. The different places he finds himself in give an unexpected range of emotional opportunities and the chance to grow up as well as to learn about life and history on the way. The experiences are described with pinpoint observation of the kind of details that make the fantastical emotionally credible. Most satisfyingly, the resolution of the adventures rests on Robert's own ingenuity to bring him home.

Recommended age: 11+

Catherine Fisher
Corbenic
Red Fox

Living alone with his mother since the age of 6, Cal has learned how to cope with her drinking and occasional

fantasy

spells of madness. But now he has had enough of hiding the knives and bottles during one of her bad turns. Instead he is off to stay with his rich uncle, leaving his mother bedraggled and despairing on the station platform at Bangor. But getting off the train at the wrong place, Cal finds himself in an unfamiliar wasteland of desolation presided over by the Fisher King's mysterious castle. Cal knows that he must now return to the mother he has betrayed, but how will he escape from the strange and often dangerous country he has blundered into?

This excellent story is a reworking of the Grail legend, in which a young knight has to seek out the mysterious magic cup that holds the key to the rebirth of nature from sterility and death. In this story, Cal has to work both with traditional symbols such as a sword, spear and stone while still retaining his knowledge of the modern world he has come from. His quest to put things right in this unfamiliar universe merges with his feeling that he has not done the right thing by his own mother. As in other epic stories, his various struggles against external enemies are accompanied by an increasing understanding of his own personal strengths and weaknesses. The author has a fine track record in writing fantasy that links the old with the new. This

fantasy

story, with its chapter headings drawn from ancient sources but with Cal himself an utterly modern character, is one of her best.

Recommended age: 11+

Jackie French
Hitler's Daughter
Collins

To amuse themselves as they wait for the school bus, a group of children from the Australian outback tell themselves stories: stories of aliens, fairies, dinosaurs or anything else that comes to mind. But, one day, Anna starts a story about Hitler's daughter. While Ben scoffs at any story about Hitler that doesn't involve bombs and Brownshirts, Mark, Little Tracey and Anna herself are drawn into the make-believe. What if Hitler did have a daughter? Who was she and what would it feel like to be her?

In Anna's story, Heidi is kept shut away in a grand house in the country where she's looked after by the kindly Fraulein Gelber. Even though she doesn't call him father, Heidi knows that Hitler, who comes to visit her from time to time, is her father – just as she knows that the disfiguring birthmark on her face and her lame leg set her apart from the pure Aryan race that her father is determined to create. No wonder he keeps her a secret. But Heidi is just a daughter who loves her father and longs to help him, knowing nothing of the hideous truth of what he has done until the final

fantasy

moments when she meets him in the bunker and sees him for the last time.

Mark is captivated by Anna's story, which provokes him to think about how it would feel to have parents who did things that were evil. Would you still love them? *Hitler's Daughter* skilfully weaves history and fantasy together to create an original story about Hitler and the atrocities of World War II that asks important questions about families and their responsibilities.

Recommended age: 11+

Lian Hearn
Across the Nightingale Floor
Macmillan

Set in a timeless Japan where feudal lords hold sway and life is regarded as cheap compared to the value of honour and bravery, *Across the Nightingale Floor* is an exciting and violent story of love, loyalty and betrayal. Raised among the Hidden, a peaceful tribe scratching out a simple living in the countryside, Tomasu knows little of the way of life of the warlords and their followers who live beyond the jungle that encloses his village. But all that changes when his home is burnt to the ground and his mother is killed. Tomasu's own life is saved by Lord Otori who adopts him as a son and sweeps him off to his stronghold where he is propelled into a new world of incredible intrigue and danger. Tomasu must learn the rituals of courtly life, he must understand the complex codes of honour and, above

fantasy

all, he must keep the secret of Lord Otori's alliance with Lady Maruyama. By making use of the magical skills he has inherited from the Tribe, Tomasu watches and listens. Quick to recognize danger and to know whom to trust, he swiftly sees what lies hidden behind rituals, sensing the trickery that threatens Lord Otori and may end his own life.

Carried by a tightly structured plot, *Across the Nightingale Floor* is also a book of powerful emotions and great tenderness.

Recommended age: 11+

Mary Hoffman
Stravaganza: City of Masks
Bloomsbury

Lucien, recovering from a near-fatal illness, finds himself transported back four centuries to Bellezza, an imaginary town very similar to Venice. He is in fact a 'stravagante' – someone who can transport himself in space as well as time. He soon learns of a plot to assassinate the Duchessa – the female leader who never seems to get any older. More uncomfortably, it

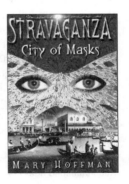

seems that Lucien has been specially picked out to save the whole city. With the help of fishermen, gondoliers

fantasy

and other locals, he manages to get by, with his own health still a serious problem. But with two more stories yet to go in this trilogy, nothing can be taken for granted in a world where intrigue and murder seem a way of life and there is the endless plotting of one faction against another in the search for ultimate power.

> **66** In a room at the top of a tall house overlooking a canal, a man sat dealing cards on to a desk covered in black silk. **99**

This book is the genuine stuff of fantasy, swapping today's place and time for another period where everything is much more dramatic as well as dangerous. It is full of passion and movement, and there is never a dull moment as youthful heroes and heroines battle against older, craftier but finally over-ambitious enemies. Set in an imaginary Italy, it conveys all the excitement of another country where emotions often run high, colours seem more gorgeous and there is an artistic heritage second to none.

Inspired by a trip made by the author to Venice, this story should involve anyone who has yet to visit that magical city. They can do the next best thing by reading about a place so very similar in this lively, cleverly crafted novel.

Recommended age: 11+

fantasy

Lesley Howarth

MapHead

Walker

Twelve-year-old MapHead is so called because he can make any map appear on to his own hairless head at a moment's notice. He possesses this and other unearthly skills because he is the son of Powers, an alien from the Subtle World that co-exists side by side with our own. But MapHead's mother is an ordinary human being, and he has now come back to her. She knows nothing about her strange child, with all memories of the events that led to his birth wiped away by Powers in order to save her sanity. MapHead tracks her down by taking on human form and going to school locally, where he soon becomes friends with his half-brother Kenny. He then has to decide whether he is going to stay for good or else continue his journeying across different worlds with his devoted father.

Aliens in space fiction often have little personality beyond their various special needs and effects. MapHead is an exception. He is confused in a very human way about his divided loyalties to both parents, and his touching and gently amusing story shows how he sets about managing earthly routines such as

fantasy

shopping and going to school. He also has to cope with an aggressive traffic warden who later turns out to be his grandmother. Living with his father in a greenhouse where they can see but not be seen, mixing acts of magic with everyday normality, battling to understand his own complex emotions, MapHead himself comes over as utterly real.

Lesley Howarth is a brilliant writer, making the unbelievable seem almost normal after only a few pages. This story is one of her finest.

Recommended age: 13+

Brian Jacques
Redwall Series
Red Fox

This fabulous series, now comprising fifteen volumes and still with no end in sight, is set in and around Redwall Abbey, somewhere in the imaginary Mossflower country. It is home to a community of English-speaking mice, periodically in danger from equally conversational rats, lizards, ferrets and various other traditional baddies of the animal world. Written with huge energy and featuring characters who often talk in dialect, adventures come thick

fantasy

and fast in books that mix verse with prose as one heroic climax is followed in quick succession by another and then another. Main characters have an obliging tendency to tell readers exactly who they are and what they are thinking, and there is always exciting action to look forward to. Everything else in these stirring tales also tends to be happily over the top, with sunny summers invariably giving way to freezing winters, made bearable by the regular arrival of enormous feasts that sometimes take as many days to prepare as to eat. Brian Jacques' fans range from the very young to the adult, all fascinated by his lavishly described other world.

Recommended age: 11+

Ursula Le Guin
A Wizard of Earthsea

Puffin

As rich in language and imagery as it is in imagination, *A Wizard of Earthsea* is an irresistible journey into another time and place. Earthsea, a world of wizards and magic, is one of the finest of all fictional fantasy lands. Here Duny, a motherless young boy growing up wild on the Island of Gont, shows that he has the magic powers that mark him out as a future wizard or 'madge'. At 13, Duny must leave his home and his old life behind him. Renamed 'Ged', he begins to learn of his own powers before he is sent to the school for wizards on the Island of Roke. Even among the other chosen young wizards, Ged's powers are proved to be

fantasy

exceptional but, as with many other novices in these arts, his arrogance leads him close to overstepping his powers when he is challenged to raise the dead – almost killing himself in the process.

A Wizard of Earthsea is perfectly realized in details of place, which create a flawlessly constructed world. Against this setting, Ursula Le Guin weaves a story that is seeped in mythology as well as crisp with magic. Full of warnings about the nature of power and its ability to corrupt, it also celebrates the triumph of good over evil.

Recommended age: 11+

Margaret Mahy
Alchemy
Flamingo

Although Roland has good looks, enough money, success at school and a beautiful girl-friend, he comes close to sacrificing everything when he is caught shoplifting. Unable to work out quite what came over him, he is then blackmailed by a sinister teacher into finding out more about his fellow-pupil, the friendless Jess Ferret. But when Roland visits Jess at home he blunders into a quite different world of mystery, menace and magic. Both he and Jess find they

fantasy

have access to another universe of terrible danger mixed with extraordinary forces. To make matters worse, others are after both them and their new powers. Still trying to live the exterior life of an ordinary schoolboy, Roland has to overcome one final challenge that threatens both him and Jess with extinction. This also happens just at the moment when they begin a love affair that is deeper than either would ever have believed possible.

> **So here it was again – coming through the dark at him – the dream, the nightmare that had haunted him for years.**

Margaret Mahy is an amazing writer. She describes adolescence not just as it is but also in terms of various supernatural events that mirror what is going on within a teenager's sometimes turbulent thoughts and feelings. The strong feelings Roland and Jess have for each other are also described in terms of possession by a magic spell. Mysterious external powers are pushing Roland within his own mind – very much as real adolescents sometimes feel taken over by forces they don't fully understand. Sometimes scary, at other moments passionate, this novel offers a voyage into the unknown that is also at the same time strangely familiar. The author has never written a bad book for teenagers; this is one of her best.

Recommended age: 11+

fantasy

Jan Mark
The Eclipse of the Century
Scholastic

When the articulated truck hits him, Keith expects to die. Instead, he is greeted by long-haired men and women who promise him that they'll meet him again 'in Kantoom, under the black sun, at the end of a thousand years'. With only nine months to go until the end of the century, Keith begins a frantic search that will take him to the meeting that must be his destiny. Arriving at Qantoum, a town in the middle of the Asian desert with a distinctly post-Soviet aura (which no one has ever heard of and which is no longer what it once was), Keith meets an eccentric cast of characters – including the Joggers for Jesus, the New Agers, the strange Mrs Fahrenheit and Lieutenants Kije and Fitzgibbon, who greet him at the station and subject him to a series of Kafkaesque exchanges that reveal little but lead him on his journey towards the new century.

" As Near Death Experiences go it had been irregular, as he discovered when he read up on the subject afterwards. "

fantasy

The Eclipse of the Century is a teasing and tantalizing glimpse of an original future that unfolds with a crackling vibrancy. Puzzling, witty and always unexpected, the story is told in such careful detail that Keith's dreamlike journey becomes the reader's too. The future it creates is full of recognizable reality as well as some frightening insights into what may actually happen.

Recommended age: 13+

Garth Nix
Sabriel
Collins

Eighteen-year-old Sabriel is in her last year at a posh boarding school. A ghostly visitation in the dormitory one night tells her that because her famous magician father has disappeared, it is she who now has the duty of banishing zombies back to the nether world where they belong. This is not easy, since they are also expert in taking on the appearance of living people, giving Sabriel some nasty surprises on the way. Supported only by a cat of dubious loyalty and a handsome young man she has brought back to life from a spell, Sabriel has to make a terrifying journey past the nine gates of the river that divides the living from the dead in the hope of rescuing her father. Her story ends on a dramatic if uncertain note, with two more volumes still to come.

This is a superb book. Among many other would-be fantasy authors, Garth Nix stands out by the force of

fantasy

his writing and the ingenious way he mixes fantasy with hard reality. At some stages this story could have been set in Britain one hundred years ago. At other times, its descriptions of slave labour camps are painfully reminiscent of the various dictatorships that arose during the twentieth century. The whole idea of one, solitary figure having to save civilization from take-over by an evil empire makes for a highly dramatic story. Garth Nix never puts a foot wrong in this absorbing fantasy, which already has as many adult as it does younger fans.

Recommended age: 11+

George Orwell
Animal Farm
Penguin

Things are in such a mess at Manor Farm that the animals finally decide to take over. Led by two pigs, Napoleon and Snowball, they drive out their corrupt master Mr Jones and resolve that from now on all animals will work together for the common good and be treated equally. Boxer, a huge carthorse, works particularly hard. But he is disturbed when Napoleon reveals one day that he has been secretly training some puppies to become vicious

George Orwell Animal Farm

fantasy

guard dogs. They finally chase away Snowball, Napoleon's chief rival as leader, and after that nothing goes right. The loyal Boxer toils harder than ever, but there are still food shortages that affect everyone except Napoleon. Finally, when Boxer is old and exhausted, he is bundled off to the slaughterhouse. Meanwhile Napoleon is becoming friendly again with Mr Jones. When the now enslaved farm animals gaze through the window at their current and former unjust bosses dining together, 'it was impossible to say which was which.'

> **'A bird's wing, comrades,' he said, 'is an organ of propulsion and not of manipulation. It should therefore be regarded as a leg. The distinguishing mark of a Man is the hand, the instrument with which he does all his mischief.'**

The author loathed the communist system ruling Russia, and this bitter satire is among the most effective attacks ever made upon it. Napoleon stands for Stalin, the evil Russian dictator, while Snowball is his great rival Trotsky, whom Stalin had murdered after driving him into exile. The guard dogs are Stalin's secret police, while Boxer stands for all the betrayed Russian workers, many of whom were treated with extreme viciousness under Stalin's regime. This fable can simply be read as a brilliant and gripping story. But knowing the history behind it reveals what a masterpiece it is, with the author in just over a hundred pages managing to paint

fantasy

a genuinely tragic as well as unforgettable picture of a political system that promised much and delivered little.

Recommended age: 11+

Mervyn Peake
Titus Groan
Vintage

Titus Groan is the first novel in the *Gormenghast* trilogy, Mervyn Peake's elaborate Gothic fantasy in which he creates a fabulous and claustrophobic world of grotesque and incredible characters against the background of the massive castle-kingdom of Gormenghast.

> 66 The walls of the vast room, which were streaming with calid moisture, were built with grey slabs of stone and were the personal concern of a company of eighteen men known as the 'Grey Scrubbers'. 99

Gormenghast is a labyrinth of a place from its cellars to its turrets, with obscure corners, hidden cloisters and endless stairways and passages. *Titus Groan* begins on the eighth day of the eighth month when the 'New One' is born – the new male heir to the Groan family. Although there is no immediate question of succession, his very birth is seen as a challenge since it is a form of change – not something welcomed at Gormenghast.

fantasy

Titus is born to be the seventeenth earl of Groan, which means he will inherit Gormenghast when his father, the current earl, dies. But Titus's father is not actually in charge of Gormenghast, rather it is Sourdust, the lord of the library and the keeper of Groan lore, and his son Barquentine, who control the ritual and ceremony that underpin everything that happens.

In the highly structured society of Gormenghast, everyone has a position and a clearly defined character. Mervyn Peake describes their physical characteristics, their habits, and their personal foibles in the smallest detail. Even the food that is eaten is itemised exactly. All of this contributes to creating the intricate and complex world with its myriad conventions that lies at the heart of *Titus Groan*. The *Gormenghast* trilogy continues with *Gormenghast* and *Titus Alone*.

Recommended age: 15+

Terry Pratchett
The Colour of Magic
Corgi

Terry Pratchett's bestselling *Discworld* series begins with *The Colour of Magic,* which introduces the extraordinary world that exists on the disc that four elephants hold up on the back of Great A'Tuin, a giant Turtle. It's a crazy world of magic and adventure with a cast of thousands where nothing is quite what it seems. At the heart of Discworld lie the twin cities of Ankh and Morpork, one proud and successful, the other full

fantasy

of crime and poverty. Here live a vast cast of characters from trolls (who are 'silicaceous life forms'), dragons who exist only if you believe in them, picture imps and Rincewind, the wizard who cannot remember any spells except the one that it is too dangerous to use. Visiting Ankh-Morpork comes Twoflower, the first tourist to this strange place. And he's hardly usual himself especially as he comes with luggage that talks and runs around on little feet. What happens on his visit to Discworld is unpredictable, illogical, fast, furious and very funny.

Terry Pratchett writes with enormous vigour, piling images on top of each other to create a multi-layered world in the richest of vocabularies. He demands careful reading just to keep up with the action but it's worth it to enter into his fabulous creation. The story of Twoflower's travels is continued in the next Discworld title, *The Light Fantastic*.

Recommended age: 13+

Philip Pullman
Northern Lights
Scholastic

From the opening moments of *Northern Lights*, the first in Philip Pullman's prize-winning trilogy *His Dark Materials*, there is a powerful sense of a grand-scale story about to unfold. Lyra Belacqua lives a life of charmed freedom among the scholars of Jordan College, Oxford, but everything changes when Lord

fantasy

Asriel, famous explorer and experimental theologian, returns from his travels in the north. From him Lyra hears stories of violent uprising and learns of worlds far beyond the Oxford she knows. Curious, and even more so after she's met the mesmerising Mrs Coulter, Lyra is swept away to London. Here Lyra is at first entranced, but later terrified, as she discovers Mrs Coulter's chilling secret. Guided by her dæmon Pantalaimon, Lyra steers a way through the dangers before embarking on a journey to the frozen north, a land of armoured bears and the witch-clans of the Arctic, where she plays a heroic role in the struggle for life itself.

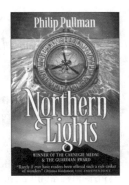

Northern Lights is an exciting, original and richly imagined story of survival. Pullman creates a new world, one that is comfortably familiar but which has distinct and important differences from real life. *Northern Lights* is no simple struggle between the powers of good and bad; Pullman's characters are capable of changing. The author describes the message of his book in powerful terms: 'We have to grow up and leave childhood; our task is to become wise and to leave our innocence behind,' he writes. 'That means engaging with our bodies and a reverence for this life here on this earth; making moral choices that involve compromise

fantasy

because we're usually involved with competing goods, not a good and a bad.' *Northern Lights* is followed by *The Subtle Knife* and *The Amber Spyglass*.

Recommended age: 11+

Joan G. Robinson
When Marnie Was There
HarperCollins

Nothing right seems to happen to young Anna. Living in a foster home after both parents have died, she has no friends and little enjoyment of life. Her kindly foster mother thinks that a spell in the country with relations might bring her out of her unnaturally passive state, and so Anna starts on the holiday of a lifetime. Very soon she makes friends with Marnie, a girl her own age who lives nearby. But there is something strange about Marnie, and after she disappears Anna begins to wonder whether she has simply imagined her. Anna has by now made friends with other children from a large, neighbouring family, and together they read an old diary which reveals that Marnie was indeed real but had lived in the same place many years earlier.

> **" Anna and the girl eyed each other in the half light. 'Are you real?' Anna whispered at last. 'Yes, are you?' "**

This beautiful novel, written in 1967, has long been a favourite. The whole notion of an ideal friendship has

fantasy

always appealed to young people. When this perfect relationship is also formed across time there is the added excitement and mystery of the impossible just for a while actually happening. Set in a Norfolk village near the sea, this story mixes nostalgia for a now lost way of life with the psychological realities of a girl on the brink of adolescence who has to learn once again how to trust others in order to have the sort of life she really wants. Lively at times, wistful at others, this story is one of those classics that finds new readers in every succeeding generation.

Recommended age: 11+

Paul Stewart and Chris Riddell
Beyond The Deepwoods
Corgi

The first in the *Edge Chronicles*, stories set in the fantastical land that juts right out into the sea, *Beyond The Deepwoods* tells of life at the origins of the great Edgewater River right in the heart of the Deepwoods. Here woodtrolls, slaughterers, gyle goblins and many others live a hard life full of danger, from the monstrous creatures who may invade their territory as well as from the flesh-eating trees that grow there. Once outside the Deepwoods there are other dangers, too. There are the Edgelands, the Twilight Woods, the Mire – all magical and all places to be reckoned with.

It is into this world that Twig is born. Abandoned at birth by his mother, Twig is brought up by a family of woodtrolls. But sooner or later Twig must set out to

fantasy

find his own destiny and his true self. His journey is a quest fraught with danger but he survives, helped by many, but also thanks to his intelligence and empathy. Twig learns that you must trust your own judgement – appearances are deceptive – and that that you must ask questions to find out the truth. Armed with this knowledge, he proves to be a resourceful and attractive hero. Rich in nonsensical invention in text and illustrations alike, and held together by a powerful sense of place, the *Edge Chronicles* are a continuing saga imbued with an unusual and charming kindness.

Recommended age: 11+

J.R.R. Tolkien
The Lord of the Rings
HarperCollins

Numbering over a thousand pages, this trilogy – comprising *The Fellowship of the Ring*, *The Two Towers* and *The Return of the King* – is the most famous sequence of fantasy fiction ever written. Its main character, Frodo, has the enormous responsibility of first locating and then returning the mysterious ring of the title to where it can never be found again. This task is vital, since in the wrong hands the ring confers limitless powers for evil. To fulfil his mission, Frodo must trek across whole continents inhabited by elves, dwarves, dragons, wizards, orcs, goblins, talking trees plus hosts of other menacing enemies of all shapes and sizes. On his side are the few trusty friends he sets out with, and also Gandalf, the wise but now elderly wizard. Against him are a savage mountain range that has to be crossed, constant harassment from those who want to secure the ring for themselves and finally his own temporary unwillingness to get rid of his great prize when the moment of decision arrives.

Stories about epic journeys often have the advantage of moving on briskly from one adventure to another. Such is the case here, with Frodo and his friends having no time for the boring, domestic things of life since they must always press on to the next challenge. Noble, brave and resourceful, they stand for all living beings at their best, just as their enemies show the pitiless and terrifying face of evil at its most depraved. In between all the violent action there are passages celebrating the beauty of the countryside, and other moments that recall the

fantasy

devastation and horror the author witnessed as a soldier serving in the trenches during World War I. Half real, half magical, this is a story about loyalty, courage and self-knowledge under testing conditions. So powerful is the writing that reading this immense tale is like participating in Frodo's great quest yourself.

Recommended age: 11+

Diana Wynne Jones
The Merlin Conspiracy
Collins

Roddy Hyde, teenage daughter of two wizards, lives in a universe of magic and ritual. Nick Mallory, aged around 15, comes from the normal world. But their lives gradually become entwined when Roddy discovers a conspiracy whereby some thoroughly unpleasant witches and wizards are out to seize power. When Nick finds himself travelling through different, magical universes, he meets the only person that can prevent this evil take-over. A vast cast of other characters also make up this long, sprawling novel, each chapter of which bursts with new ideas. Sometimes events are reminiscent of what goes on in our own world; at other times, they soar away into another universe where everything that happens is new and strange.

> ❝ **The first thing I noticed about this person was that he had a little blue flame sitting on his forehead. 'Oh good,' I said. 'You must be a wizard.'** ❞

The author is expert in making the unbelievable seem not just possible but sometimes plain ordinary. She manages this because her characters always remain understandable in human terms, however weird their appearance and particular habits. At the back of all her work is a strong belief in the power of individuals to find their own way, whatever the obstacles they may

encounter. Of all modern fantasy writers, Diana Wynne Jones has the most wide-ranging imagination, sometimes drawing on myth and legend, at other times moving with complete confidence around worlds entirely of her own making.

Recommended age: 11+

John Wyndham
The Midwich Cuckoos
Penguin

During the whole of September 27, everyone living in the little village of Midwich was asleep. Anyone trying to visit the village was affected in the same way. There were also rumours of an unfamiliar object seen overhead. Nine months later the sixty-one women in the village of childbearing age all have babies who are

fantasy

perfectly normal except for their strange, golden eyes. Living slightly apart from the rest of the village, the children spend all their time with each other, finally choosing to move permanently into the local school specially set up for them. But when an ordinary young villager is killed after one of the children fixes him with a piercing gaze, it becomes evident that these are visitors from another planet, out to colonize first the village and then the rest of the world.

This story is far more than a clever exercise in tension and suspense. It also reflects the general unease adults can feel as children grow up and start doing things their own way – sometimes in direct contradiction to what their parents and teachers want and expect. Those adults in power within Midwich are finally faced by the appalling dilemma of whether to kill all these mutant children off while there is still the chance. *The Midwich Cuckoos* has continued to haunt generations of readers ever since it was first published in 1957.

Recommended age: 11+

fantasy

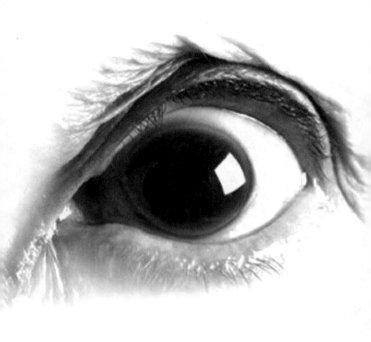

horror

Iain Banks
The Wasp Factory
Abacus

Sixteen-year-old Frank Cauldhame tells the story of his life partly from his immediate perspective and partly through the immature half-truths of his younger self. In both voices Iain Banks writes in a jaunty descriptive style that draws the reader effortlessly into a story of escalating violence and increasing sickness. Banks's strong sense of place, his ability to evoke the windswept coastal landscape, gives a disturbing reality to the many-layered story that Frank unfolds.

Frank lives with his crippled father on a semi-island, far from prying eyes but with the ever-present threat of his deranged brother returning home. Frank is a loner who has created his own world shored up by his own private mythology; a world of special – usually bloody – places with the Wasp Factory and the Sacrifice Poles at its heart. He boasts of having already killed three people and describes each death with a cold detachment. The deaths of people are just a tack-on to his arbitrary slaughter of animals, including an especially savage revenge killing of rabbits.

Frank is a horribly credible character and his gruesome behaviour is perfectly convincing. Unlocking the secret of the trauma that haunts him is just another macabre twist in this chilly but compelling tale.

Recommended age: 15+

horror

Melvin Burgess
Bloodtide

London is in ruins, ruled over by two mobsters and their families, both out for ultimate control. One of them, Val Vonson, offers his 14-year-old daughter Signy in marriage to his younger rival Conor. This is only a stalling device to enable Vonson to complete his plans for domination, and Signy wants nothing to do with it. But when she realizes Conor truly loves

her, she softens for a time before more fighting between the two factions drives them apart. In an act of terrible cruelty, Conor has both her legs broken in order to keep her from running away from the tower where he wants her to stay. Signy sets about planning her revenge, which when it comes is equally savage. But by this time, alienated from the son she bore as well as from her beloved twin brother, she knows she has also killed something in herself. Her story ends violently, with no sign that the next generation has learned anything from all this horror.

This is one of the most violent books ever written for a younger audience. But by basing it closely on an ancient Icelandic saga, its controversial author could fairly claim that he was merely bringing an old, savage myth to new life. He does this brilliantly, although readers will certainly need strong stomachs when it comes to some of the acts of cruelty scattered throughout this narrative. The London of the future imagined here is equally appalling, consisting of violent rulers, strange hybrid half-men and any number of other grotesque mutations. But there is still some good to be found, even in this brutish existence. The tension in this novel never lets up until its last blood-soaked pages have come and gone, leaving readers with plenty to think about afterwards – and perhaps a few nightmares.

Recommended age: 13+

Roald Dahl
Skin and Other Stories
Puffin

A woman who kills her husband with a leg of lamb? A sound machine that can hear a plant crying? A man with a work of art tattooed on his back so perfect that dealers can't wait to get their hands on it? The adventures of a priceless diamond accidentally swallowed by a burglar? Yes, we are in Roald Dahl territory, but this time he is writing for older readers. One of these stories, *The Champion of the World*, was a first draft for a later novel for children, and another, *Beware of the Dog*, draws on his own experience of suffering a serious air crash. Beautifully written and always finishing at exactly the moment when nothing more need be said, these stories

horror

are sometimes horrific but always darkly amusing. More examples of the same skill can be found in two further collections: *The Wonderful World of Henry Sugar* and *The Great Automatic Grammatizator*.

Although Dahl wrote mainly to amuse, many of the subjects he felt seriously about also appear regularly in his fiction. He hated the bullying he had encountered at his boarding school, and in one of these stories, *Galloping Foxley*, he paints an unforgettable portrait of this vicious behaviour at its worst. Dahl was also fascinated by marriage, both those that remain happy and the other sort, where husband and wife may end up loathing each other enough even to turn to murder. But above everything else, Dahl loved teasing his readers, often cleverly leading them down one fictional path when all the time they should have been looking down another. What an entertainer!

Recommended age: 13+

Neil Gaiman
Coraline
Bloomsbury

Coraline is bored. Her parents, who both work at home, are too busy to have much to do with her during the holidays. The occupants of the flats above and below are nice enough but rather weird. So Coraline sets about exploring the old house that she and her parents have just moved into, and in particular a mysterious door that leads to nowhere. But one day she finds the key and enters into a similar house that also contains two people very much like her own parents. But there is something wrong about them, in particular their black button eyes and habit of eating beetles. And when Coraline wants to return to her proper home, her new mother tells her that this will be possible only if she can solve a particular problem. This task has already defeated three other previously kidnapped children, who now exist as ghosts in what turns out to be a prison rather than an alternative home.

This spooky tale reads like a modern version of Lewis Carroll's *Alice* stories, but this time containing far more of the nightmare element. Yet Coraline herself is an equally determined small girl, well able to hold her own in a new world of singing rats and talking cats. The deadly guessing game she is forced to play by her new mother is both entertaining and frightening, given the ever-present threat to Coraline herself. The author is better known as the creator of the famous *Sandman* comic strip, later turned into a renowned series of graphic novels. This story is a new development for him, combining scary details, such as hands that scuttle across the floor, with a sensitive description of how a brave child still manages to get the better of a truly formidable enemy dressed up in the body of a trusted parent.

Recommended age: 13+

horror

Nick Gifford
Piggies
Puffin

After getting lost in an old quarry Ben finds himself transplanted to another world very much like his own but with one fatal difference. Everyone there is a vampire, drinking each other's blood often and with relish. So when a new, unfamiliar source of nourishment such as Ben himself wanders into their midst, they can hardly believe their luck. Faced with a lifetime of imprisonment for the purposes of regular blood giving, Ben manages to escape to a group of others like him, also in perpetual danger from the bloodsuckers. But he is soon recaptured, and this time finds himself kept in a secure unit along with other 'piggies', the name given to those humans kept only for their blood. Ben escapes again, with the help of the one person within this horrifying existence willing to help him. They just make it back to Ben's world, but there is still one more stinging surprise to come.

> 66 At first he had thought she was scared; terrified to find herself in a strange new world. But no. That wasn't fear in her eyes. It was something else. Rachel was excited. And Rachel was hungry... 99

Horror stories frequently have a way of bringing to the surface anxieties that many people have (often without realizing it), but there is more to this artfully

horror

written story than mere horror. *Piggies* also reveals what it must be like to be an animal in a factory farm, should such an animal also possess human sensibilities. And even if animals don't always know what is happening to them, there is enough here to rouse both pity and disgust at what they have to endure under modern factory farming methods. But this book is no simple vegetarian text. It also highlights the way in which those who don't belong to any ruling group can quickly become victims of their oppressors. Or as one character puts it, 'Treat a person like an animal and they'll behave like one.'

Recommended age: 11+

Susan Hill
The Woman in Black
Vintage

Arthur Kripps is a young solicitor when he is sent to Eel Marsh House to sort out the will of the late Mrs Alice Drablow. He sets off on the trip in high spirits, believing it to be a simple business matter and looking forward to nothing more taxing than the train ride and a visit to

horror

the countryside. What he doesn't know is that the trip will change his life for ever.

It is at Mrs Drablow's funeral that Arthur first sees the creepy woman in black. She is so gaunt that her skin is stretched across her face with the bones showing through underneath. She disappears immediately after the burial and, when Arthur makes enquiries of her in the local town, he finds no one willing to talk about her. Furthermore, the locals all advise him against staying in Eel Marsh House to complete his business. But with the bravado of youth, Arthur stays the night and soon becomes the victim of the sinister presence that haunts it.

> 66 And then, from somewhere within the depths of the house – but somewhere not very far from the room in which I was – I heard a noise. It was a faint noise, and, strain my ears as I might, I could not make out exactly what it was. 99

horror

Telling the story as an older man looking back on his life, Arthur reveals the truth behind the woman in black and the chilling price he pays for meeting her. Susan Hill creates an atmosphere of terror as Arthur discovers an empty rocking chair that is still rocking in the locked nursery and hears the pitiful scream of a child drowning out on the marshes. *The Woman in Black* is a classic ghost story with a horrific twist, in which the tension is maintained till the very last.

Recommended age: 15+

Stephen King
Carrie
New English Library

Sixteen-year-old Carrie is the girl whom everyone mocks at school. Clumsy, badly dressed, hopeless at games, and with a mother who is a religious maniac, she is a natural target. But an already bad situation gets completely out of hand one day in the showers after a game of volleyball. The other girls round on Carrie so savagely that many are afterwards ashamed of their cruelty. Encouraged by a teacher who saw what was going on, a fellow-pupil, Susan Snell, tries to make amends. She gets her attractive boyfriend Tommy to take Carrie to the final school dance. But the mean Chris Hargensen, always the nastiest to Carrie, has other ideas. Carrie's social triumph is cruelly wrecked; in return, she takes a truly terrible revenge.

Carrie has the power of telekinesis – she can make physical objects move simply by wishing it. So when she comes to believe that the entire school community was out to humiliate her all along, her response is to destroy as many of them as possible. Stephen King makes all this believable by writing his book as if it is

horror

made up from assorted case-notes, journalism and personal diaries. He also has strong sympathy for Carrie, so that she never comes over simply as a stage villain. Only at the end, when presiding gleefully over all the destruction, does she become a truly horrific character. Before that, it is some of the other girls and Carrie's own mother who seem genuinely evil, which uses strong language and has an underlying sexual take on much that happens. This compelling, uneasy book was also made into an unforgettable film.

Recommended age: 13+

Darren Shan
Cirque du Freak
Collins

Stealing a poisonous spider is not the kind of thing a schoolboy often does, but when Darren Shan sees Madam Octa he knows he must have her. What he can't predict are the consequences. Darren is caught up in a struggle for life itself and must make a pact with a vampire to save his friend's life.

Everyone warns Darren not to go to the Cirque du Freak. His teachers tell him it's a disgusting idea and his parents agree. But to Darren and his friends the chance of seeing a snake boy or a wolf man is irresistible – even though the tickets are very expensive and mysteriously difficult to get hold of. Sneaking out late at night, Darren and his best friend Steve make their way to the old broken-down theatre where the show is to be held. From the first moment, nothing is quite

horror

what they expect. How does Mr Tall know Darren's name, for example? Once inside, they are awed by the strange characters that they see, but nothing prepares them for Mr Crepsley and his horrifying spider. Controlled by Mr Crepsley's flute, Madam Octa stuns a live goat on stage and then spins a web off Mr Crepsley's lips. It's scary stuff, but what's even more scary is that Steve wants to talk to him at the end. Overhearing their conversation, Darren discovers that there's something very unusual about his friend – and it's not good. *Cirque du Freak* is the first in a compelling series.

Recommended age: 11+

Robert Louis Stevenson
The Strange Case of Dr Jekyll and Mr Hyde
Penguin

Dr Jekyll seems an entirely admirable man, but he is troubled by the darker side of his personality. So he invents a drug that will separate the good and bad sides of his nature for ever. When he drinks this potion he literally turns into someone else, in this case the sneering, evil figure of Mr Hyde. After stalking about Edinburgh causing as much upset as he

horror

213

can, this malevolent individual eventually changes back into good Dr Jekyll, who can continue his life untempted by the sort of bad behaviour now indulged in only by his other half. But Dr Jekyll soon finds it increasingly hard to return from being Mr Hyde; he also sometimes slips into this loathsome figure without being able to stop himself. With his supply of drugs running out and Mr Hyde being pursued by the police, the poor doctor finds himself in a nightmarish and unbearable predicament.

> 66 My mind submerged in terror. 'O God!' I screamed, and 'O God!' again and again; for there before my eyes – pale and shaken, and half fainting, and groping before him with his hands, like a man restored from death – there stood Henry Jekyll! 99

This short story caused immediate interest when it was published in 1886, with the phrase 'Jekyll and Hyde' soon entering the language as a way of describing someone who can behave in totally contradictory ways. Psychologists were also interested in this story, given that people trying to come to terms with their own destructive side would sometimes deny its existence altogether, as if – like Jekyll – they were talking about somebody else rather than themselves. The author believed that humans have to learn how to balance every part of their personality as best they can. In this powerful story he shows the terrible consequences that can follow when individuals deliberately distance

horror

themselves from their bad side rather than trying to understand what is happening and if necessary seeking help.

Recommended age: 13+

Bram Stoker
Dracula
Penguin

Bram Stoker's *Dracula* has the unusual distinction of having been continuously in print since its publication in 1897. It is a gripping story of suspense, infused with horror. Its power has caused the name 'Dracula' to become synonymous with 'vampire', and rightly so – he is a towering and terrifying creation who instils dread wherever his name is heard.

Dracula is written as the journal entries and letters of Jonathan Harker, his fiancée Mina and their friend Dr Seward. It's a device that gives the story great immediacy and variation as well as building up the tension. Harker travels on business to Transylvania to visit Count Dracula in his fairy-tale but brooding mountain-top castle. Here he has many sinister encounters, which set him wondering about his host and what exactly is going on. Stumbling on the chapel hidden in the depths of the castle, he discovers something of the truth: Dracula lives on blood sucked from the living, having become immortal through the lives of others. These poor victims are the 'Un-Dead', and they can be finally killed only by being staked

horror

through the heart. Dracula is ruthless and cunning; he can change shape at will, becoming not only another creature – most commonly a bat or a wolf – but also transforming himself into a nebulous mist. Dracula's prey are helpless and their innocence stands in stark contrast with his evil.

Bram Stoker uses Gothic motifs of wild weather, castles, tombs, psychic powers and madness, as he relates a story uncovering the savage and partially suppressed side of human nature.

Recommended age: 15+

horror

into the future

Douglas Adams
The Hitch Hiker's Guide to the Galaxy
Tor Books

One Thursday lunchtime Earth is unexpectedly demolished to make way for a new hyperspace bypass. For Arthur Dent, who has only just seen his own house destroyed that same morning, this occurs during a session in the pub with his new friend Ford Prefect. Dent then finds himself swept up into something like a flying saucer. His only guide is a most useful book with the same title as this one. He next meets the mighty Vogon, who insists on reading him some of his dreadful verse, with Dent now a prisoner strapped to a special Poetry Appreciation chair. And there is lots more to come, including a million-gallon vat of custard, the Heart of Gold Starship, an Improbability Drive and a robot that Dent thinks is more like an electronic sulking machine.

This wilfully unpredictable and often wildly funny book is one of the most original of all science fiction stories. Written sometimes in the style of a textbook complete with scholarly notes, it teems with outlandish ideas that never become too difficult since Dent always reacts to them with the utmost common sense. Four more titles follow in what the

author describes as 'a trilogy of five'. Originally written for the radio, the dialogue always goes straight to the point, with the narrative itself quickly changing from one scene to another as one more absurd character or weird notion replaces all the many that have already gone before.

Recommended age: 15+

Neil Arksey
Playing on the Edge
Puffin

Dateline 2064. Football rules the world and its top levels have become a luxury sport owned by giant corporations. In the Super League, players and their clubs are rich beyond their wildest dreams and ordinary people can no longer afford to watch matches live; instead, they have to make do with pay-per-view entertainment. And football at this level comes at a high price for the people involved in it too. The young stars are pumped full of performance-enhancing chemicals which end up killing them, and when Easy Linker's Dad discovers the truth behind the Super League he is determined that his son should have nothing more to do with football. But playing for the Gunman Reds has been Easy's lifetime ambition, and when he is signed up by them on his thirteenth birthday, nothing is going to stop him. Although Easy is determined to play football, he's also determined to find out what is happening to the country's best young players. He escapes with the information he needs, but his life is in danger and it takes all of his wits – as well as his best footballing skills – to survive.

Playing on the Edge is a thrilling adventure that raises questions about the links between sport and money and the ways in which players can become victims of the ruthlessness of business.

Recommended age: 11+

Margaret Atwood
The Handmaid's Tale
Bloomsbury

The Handmaid's Tale is set in the US in a not-too-distant future. Now called the Republic of Gilead, the country is run by a totalitarian regime basing its rule on religious principles and using the Bible to underpin its authority. Control of sexuality is one of its key tenets, especially the control of females. There is only a small pool of fertile females, known as the 'handmaidens', and they are reserved for the rulers of the Republic so that they can produce the babies of the future. The Handmaidens have no rights and no education – they are no longer even allowed to learn to read.

> 66 'There is more than one kind of freedom,' said Aunt Lydia. 'Freedom to and freedom from. In the days of anarchy, it was freedom to. Now you are being given freedom from. Don't underrate it.' 99

into the future

Offred is the handmaiden of the Commander. She knows the law and she knows, too, that she will stay alive only as long as she is capable of getting pregnant. But Offred can remember a life before this drab existence. She can remember loving her husband and playing with her daughter; she can remember when she had a job and money. Drawing on her memories and uniting other women, Offred plans rebellion.

The Handmaid's Tale is a terrifying dystopian story. Like other novels about future worlds, such as George Orwell's *Nineteen Eighty-four* or Aldous Huxley's *Brave New World*, it is a dark satire about how power corrupts and how hard it is to fight. In particular, it points out that the liberation of women is constantly under threat.

Recommended age: 15+

J.G. Ballard
The Drowned World
Gollancz

Dr Kerans and a group of scientists are in the third year of an expedition to see what can be rescued from the long-submerged world of London. Living in the top of the abandoned Ritz Hotel, Kerans finds that he and others are beginning to slip back in their mental set to those prehistoric times when once before most of the world was covered by water. When the order comes to abandon the research station, he stays behind with the beautiful Beatrice, still believing that he is better off where he is than returning to what is left of civilization. But the arrival of the sinister Strangman and his band of pirates changes everything, with Kerans and Beatrice now at greater risk than ever before.

This dark and moody story can be read on a number of different levels. As science fiction, it paints a memorable picture of a rotting, underwater world infested by iguanas and salamanders in the glare of an ever-stronger sun. But it is also a reworking of the Garden of Eden story, with Kerans a modern Adam let loose in dense vegetation which, however threatening, is somehow safer and more wholesome than the human world elsewhere. Creating an unforgettable picture, this novel is one of many futuristic stories by J.G. Ballard. Drawn towards images of desolation and disaster, he is still one of the most original of all contributors to this particular genre. Those who enjoy this story should also read his fine *Vermilion Sands* series, which once again combines a black vision of the future with a more general feeling of ultimate timelessness.

Recommended age: 15+

Julie Bertagna
Exodus
Macmillan

Mara knows that her island home is doomed. With the mighty icecaps of the North steadily melting down, storms and subsequent floods are becoming ever more threatening. And she also has had a glimpse of a faraway new world in her cyberwizz – one of the few pieces of advanced technology that has survived from

into the future

the past. Setting sail with others from her island, Mara does indeed eventually track down a city built high into the sky. But she also discovers that newcomers are not wanted there. Condemned to stay forever outside its walls, Mara decides to break past the vicious sea police and try her luck. She needs plenty of that both then and later on in order to survive all the other hectic adventures that come her way.

Everyone should know by now about the dangers of global warming, but it takes a novelist to make general discussion about weather change come alive in a vivid and disturbing way. And as Mara discovers, even if humans do learn how to build new cities above the gathering waves, there is always going to be the problem of fitting in everyone seeking shelter. In times of great shortages it is easy for civilized values to break down in favour of the survival of the fittest, but Mara finds an ally in fighting what she sees as the gross injustices heaped on those who most need help. Written by one of Britain's most promising younger novelists, *Exodus* is a big, ambitious and passionate story that relates to both the problems of global warming and the debate about asylum seekers.

Recommended age: 11+

into the future

224

Arthur C. Clarke

2001: A Space Odyssey

Orbit

2001 was far off into the future when this book was written in 1968, and Arthur C. Clarke's vision of space travel opened up the magical possibilities of alien life at a time when landing on the moon was only at the planning stage. But, beyond the science fiction, *2001* explores deeply felt emotions of human frailty – and the uncertainty of our place amidst the vastness of the solar system.

> 66 Down there on the crowded globe, the alarms would be flashing across the radar screens, the great tracking telescopes would be searching the skies – and history as men knew it would be drawing to a close. 99

The spaceship *Discovery* is sent off to explore Saturn, an epic journey into the unknown and one in which many things can, and do, go wrong. The reason for the mission is something dug up on the moon – a large, perfectly smooth, rectangular block some three million years old, which abruptly transmits a powerful radio signal directed at the

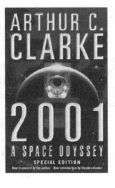

planet. In addition to the two pilots and the rest of the crew, who are in artificially induced hibernation for the journey, *Discovery* is run by the self-aware and independently minded main computer, HAL, which soon starts to take control of more than just the navigation and maintenance of the ship. The battle of wills between David Bowman, the surviving pilot, and HAL is a close-run thing, but what happens to Bowman as he reaches the end of his mission is stranger still.

Recommended age: 13+

Hal Clement
Mission of Gravity
Gollancz

Barlennan, known as a master shipman, lands his space ship *Bree* on the edge of the disc-shaped planet Mesklin. Mesklin has been a hard planet to explore as its climate is inhospitable to humans. With gravity more than 700 times greater than on Earth and temperatures so low that the oceans are liquid methane and the snow ammonia-tainted, it's not a place anyone would choose to go. But when an unmanned space probe crashes near one of Mesklin's poles, it has to be rescued, and Barlennan leads his team on the complex mission to retrieve it. Though he knows nothing of the tiny Mesklinites who can survive the harsh conditions of their planet (and have learnt to speak English), he soon finds himself relying on them to bring him and his mission to safety.

into the future

> 66 A blinding whirl of white spray and nearly white sand hid everything more than a hundred yards from the *Bree* in every direction; and now even the ship was growing difficult to see as hard-driven droplets of methane struck bullet-like and smeared themselves over his eye shells. 99

Hal Clement has created a brilliant world of the future with humans adapted to managing technology – Barlennan has pincer-tipped arms – and an alien people who are entirely civilized in their own way. *Mission of Gravity* was first published in 1954, and immediately hailed as one of the best books about the possibilities that space offers, combining scientific fact with fantasy in a creative and plausible way.

Recommended age: 15+

Philip K. Dick
Martian Time-Slip

Gollancz

Set on the desert-dry planet Mars, dateline 1994, *Martian Time-Slip* is a fast-moving story of greed and survival underpinned by the convincing and moving psychology of its characters. Established to be a place of new opportunities, the colony on Mars has already fallen into depressingly familiar patterns both of social hierarchies and corruption. With water as the key to survival, the ambitious and unscrupulous Arnie Kott,

into the future

head of the Plumbers' Union, is dangerously powerful. He will stop at nothing to achieve his own ends – including using people. Against his will, Jack Bohlen, a former schizophrenic troubled by flashbacks, finds himself working for Kott on an unusual kind of work which is distinctly distasteful.

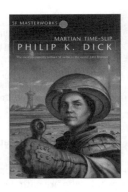

❝ From the depths of phenobarbital slumber, Silvia Bohlen heard something that called. ❞

Guiding all the efforts of those living on Mars are the frightening directives from the all-controlling UN who want to exploit the resources of the planet while also being determined that it should be a place of perfection. In their attempt to create such a place, the UN has plans to shut Camp B-G, the home for 'anomalous' children. When the father of Manfred Steiner, an autistic boy who appears to be completely shut in his own world, learns of this plan he commits suicide in despair. But Manfred turns out to have powers of seeing into the future. Jack Bohlen recognises Manfred's unusual talent, which Arnie Kott is keen to exploit as a way of making money out of the UN's future plans.

Recommended age: 15+

Ann Halam

Dr Franklin's Island

Orion

When their plane crashes onto a deserted island, the trip of a lifetime goes horribly wrong for Semi, Miranda and Arnie. Forced together by chance survival, the three struggle to keep going on the empty beach by living off fish and bananas and counting the days before rescue. It's a dangerous existence, especially living on the edge of a lagoon full of sharks, so when Arnie goes missing with his home-made raft, the two girls are grimly sure of his fate. But Arnie's disappearance is more mysterious and far more sinister than they could imagine, and soon Semi and Miranda are caught in the same trap.

All have become victims of Dr Franklin, whose secret laboratory is devoted to genetic engineering. Here he creates the most hideous mutants: pigs with human hands, monkeys with octopus legs. Semi and Miranda are to be his latest 'experiments', and he's planning rather more than physical mutation. For such sophisticated creatures, Dr Franklin devises a series of mind-games that will leave them mentally destroyed. Arnie's new form is as a snake, while Miranda's is a bird and Semi is turned into a fish – they can communicate only by drawing on strange mental powers. Somehow they must escape. *Dr Franklin's Island* is both a gripping story of friendship and survival and also a grim warning about the 'what ifs' of genetic engineering.

Recommended age: 13+

into the future

Aldous Huxley

Brave New World

Flamingo

It is the twenty-sixth century and humans have at last found a way to live peacefully with each other. Each individual is genetically fitted out for the role in life chosen for him or her by the World Controllers, who run the ten zones into which the globe is divided. The Alpha-Plus class is designed for high-flying jobs, while the Epsilon-Minus Semi-Morons are there for labouring work. A soft drug called 'soma' that brings immediate happiness is also freely prescribed. But Bernard Marx, who works at the Central London Hatchery and Conditioning Centre, is still unhappy, and his desperation to break free increases after he visits one of the few remaining Savage Reservations, where a more normal type of life – involving free choice – is still preserved. He makes friends with one of the so-called Savages, who follows him out of the electric fences that surround the reservation into the new world.

> 66 In a gap between two tunnels, a nurse was delicately probing with a long fine syringe into the gelatinous contents of a passing bottle. The students and their guides stood watching her for a few moments in silence. 99

Written in 1932, this extraordinary story seems increasingly prophetic as scientists today have advanced further towards the possibility of 'designer' babies. The author was right about many other details that have come to pass too, such as the growing availability of instantly mind-changing drugs and the 'feelies' that people attend, where what they see on the screen is compounded by accompanying physical experiences. Huxley's

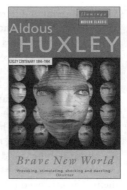

argument that happiness never comes about through technological advances alone is very persuasive. This short novel was written more as a satire than as a genuine expectation of what might happen. A later novel, *Island*, explores the whole idea of an ideal society once again, this time more sympathetically.

Recommended age: 15+

Louise Lawrence
Children of the Dust
Red Fox

From the terrifying moment when a nuclear bomb is dropped, through the long-term horrors as it affects subsequent generations, *Children of the Dust* is consistently frightening and thought-provoking. It is told as three interrelated stories by Sarah, Ophelia and

into the future

Simon, describing different kinds of survival and the morality that underpins each. Sarah's tale begins when the bomb drops out of one of the bluest skies of summer. Without her father – who is unable to get home – Sarah and the rest of her family struggle to cope, as the house and the world they live in crumble around them. The first need is for

food and water, but the effect of the bombs is far more devastating: radiation is everywhere and the fine dust that settles on everything cannot be escaped. Sarah knows her life is over, but for her younger sister Kate there is hope of survival if Johnson, a lonely and self-sufficient farmer, will take her in.

While Sarah must die, her father survives the bomb by a quirk of fate that takes him to an underground bunker. In a new life he has another daughter, Ophelia, who grows up in the confined but physically safe space. Here the military is in control, ruling the community with repressive authority while it tries to secure a future through genetic engineering. But when Ophelia dares to venture out, she finds a world of decay and mutation within which the tiny society preserved by Kate and Johnson survives through sharing and compassion – in marked contrast with her own experience. They are the future, as Simon discovers a generation later when he

into the future

finds himself in a community run not with technology but with telepathy, sympathy and tolerance.

Recommended age: 13+

Lois Lowry
The Giver
Collins

With no experience of war, hunger or pain, the citizens of this isolated Community in the future have been trained since birth to do exactly as they are told as one blameless day follows another. In order to achieve such harmony, children are taken away from their mothers at birth and then brought up by specially appointed families careful to instil all the various agreed rules of good behaviour at every opportunity. But those children who fail to come up to expectation have a way of disappearing no-one quite knows where. The same thing happens with the old, who are well cared for until each one of them goes through a special ceremony where after a final party of celebration they too are never seen again. Jonas, the teenage hero of the story, gradually finds out more about all this when he is given the job of Receiver of Memory. How he uses this painful knowledge forms the rest of this brilliant novel.

into the future

All disturbing visions of the future contain an implicit criticism of how we live now and the way that aspects of society which seem wrong at the moment could well develop into something far more sinister in time. This story focuses upon the dangers of a way of life where everyone is desperately anxious to keep in with everyone else to the extent that individuals who do not fit in are simply eliminated. It also criticizes the hypocritical use of language whereby Jonas's adopted father can still persuade himself and others that he is doing the right thing when he talks about 'releasing' difficult children when he really means killing them. Since it first appeared in 1993, this story has become a cult novel among teenagers.

Recommended age: 13+

Michael Moorcock
Behold the Man
Gollancz

Karl Glogauer is a loser – bullied at school, and self-destructive ever after. Neurotic, undisciplined and under-performing, he still tries to take comfort from his Christian beliefs. But his harsh but long-suffering girlfriend Monica tells him repeatedly that his faith is only one more of his remaining childish delusions. Intent on proving her wrong, Karl teams up with the eccentric inventor of a time machine, and travels back to Palestine in 29 AD. His aim is to meet Jesus for himself, but when he does finally manage to track him down to a small, shabby carpentry shop, Karl receives the greatest shock of his life.

Although its title is translated from the biblical phrase *ecce homo*, this book is very far from being a Christian text. It is instead an almost fiendishly intelligent, radical reworking of the Bible story, packing more into its 124 pages than many other novels do in four times the length. Alternating between the modern world and the ancient desert lands, it has ironic descriptions of the various fringe groups Karl belongs to running alongside his more taxing and memorable experiences in the company of John the Baptist. The end of this story is too good to give away but fits in entirely logically with what has come before, packing a huge emotional punch in the process. The author is rightly considered one of the best British science fiction writers, and this novel shows why. For those who want to hear more about Karl, he also features in the same author's *Breakfast in the Ruins*.

Recommended age: 15+

Robert C. O'Brien
Z For Zachariah
Puffin

Ann Burden, an American teenager, believes she's the last person left alive after a nuclear holocaust has devastated the rest of her country. Just getting by in the remote valley farm where she now lives along with a dog, a few cows and some chickens, she still mainly

into the future

wishes for human company. But when a young man appears over the horizon one day wearing a radiation-proof suit, Ann has no way of knowing whether he is going to be a friend or enemy. Her worst fears are realized when she discovers that his intention is to keep her firmly under his thumb as little more than a domestic servant. Escaping to the hills, Ann then plays a deadly game of hide and seek with someone who is determined never to grant her the individual freedom she demands.

This is a stunning book, rewriting the Garden of Eden but with Adam now turned into a sinister oppressor. It is tragic that the last two people left alive should quarrel so badly with each other, but Ann and Loomis, the young man in question, stand for more than just themselves. While Ann is a fundamentally good, conscientious person, Loomis represents all that is wrong with human beings. His urge to dominate and his lack of scruple about how he sets about doing this have to be resisted. But Ann shows that it is possible to survive without compromising her values, and so long as she can eventually find others who also think like her there is still hope. What does actually happen when this story ends is left for readers to decide for themselves. This classic novel, which never lets up on suspense for one moment, was first published in 1975 but remains just as relevant and gripping today.

Recommended age: 13+

George Orwell
Nineteen Eighty-Four
Penguin

Coming home from his work at the Ministry of Truth,
Winston Smith passes under a poster bearing an
enormous face and the slogan 'BIG BROTHER IS
WATCHING YOU.' He lives in a sordid flat in the
capital of Airstrip One, the new name for Britain and
Europe. Although any freedom of thought is instantly
punishable, he starts keeping a diary recording his
loathing of the times in which he lives. He fancies a
young woman working in his department, and
eventually they make a date – something that is also
forbidden, with the all-powerful ruling Party banning
any sexual relations outside marriage in case they lead
to individuals feeling more loyal to each other than
towards the state. After a few secret meetings, they are
both arrested. Winston is then tortured until he has lost
all sense of his own individuality. Now a broken man,
he persuades himself that he now loves Big Brother just
like everyone else.

66 The Ministry of Love was the really
frightening one. There were no windows in it at
all… it was a place impossible to enter except
on official business, and then only by penetrating through a maze of barbed-wire entangle-
ments, steel doors, and hidden machine-gun
nests. 99

into the future

The author, who wrote this book in 1948, gave it a title set in the near future as a grim warning about what might happen should essential liberties ever be lost. This was already happening in the communist take-over of Eastern Europe at the time. Orwell also drew on his experience of working for the BBC in London during the war, when government-inspired broadcasts sometimes meant that the truth came second to propaganda. But although 1984 itself has come and gone without incident, this book is still the most compelling description of what living in a total dictatorship of the future might be like. Every detail from the permitted use of language to how people are allowed to live, eat and drink is covered in writing of such conviction that to read this novel is to share the lives of the oppressed occupants of Airstrip One itself. But however depressing the ultimate message, the sheer skill and intelligence of this amazing story make it always exhilarating.

Recommended age: 15+

Susan Price
The Sterkarm Handshake
Scholastic

With the whole world open for travel, the only unexplored destination for twenty-first century holidaymakers is the past. Just down the Time Tube, it's not even very far. The sixteenth century's an exciting new territory – there's clean air, pure water, no street beggars and uncontaminated food, but, as always with time travel, there are hidden dangers. Not least the natives. For the Sterkarms, for instance, there are few home comforts. Their castle is cold and draughty, they've nothing much to keep out the rain and there are few pastimes, except riding out on raids against their neighbours. It's all perfectly normal for a border clan, and they're not unhappy with life. But then a new tribe

appears. The Elf-Folk wear funny clothes, speak in a different language and they bring dangerous gifts.

What ensues is a richly imagined and tightly constructed story, particularly when it details how the two time zones mix and mingle, and what happens when twenty-first century Andrea falls in love with Sterkarm Per. But behind the gripping love story, the drama of unequal skirmishes between sixteenth- and twenty-first-century weapons, and the life-changing effect of modern medicine, Susan Price provokes much thought about social progress – for both good and ill.

Recommended age: 11+

Philip Reeve
Mortal Engines
Scholastic

Mortal Engines is set in a wonderfully imagined

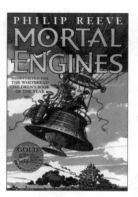

futuristic landscape amidst cities that combine a dark and sinister underworld – rivalling anything in Dickens – with exciting new technologies. London is now a mobile construction, built in tiers, criss-crossed with elevators and mounted on caterpillar tracks; other smaller, poorer cities have less sophisticated technologies, and are therefore more likely to fall victim to their powerful enemies. Against this background, the story is a fast-paced adventure, full of memorable scenes of high drama.

> 66 It was a dark, blustery afternoon in spring, and the city of London was chasing a small mining town across the dried-out bed of the old North Sea. 99

London is on the move again under the orders of Lord Mayor Crome – quite literally. Afraid of the some of the newer, hungrier and greedier cities, London has been hiding in the damp, mountainous areas of Britain. But now the time has come to set out again and chase some new prey across the Great Hunting Ground. Mounted on its giant caterpillar tracks, London joins the other cities on wheels as they charge across the

into the future

countryside, gobbling up weaker or smaller places as they go. But Crome's intentions are not entirely honourable, and it may be that only Hester and Tom, alike abandoned in the Outlands, will be able to stop him. In Hester, Tom and the courageous Katherine – a rich girl from Tier One who has to use her wits to survive when Crome double-deals her father – *Mortal Engines* depicts powerful characters whose resourcefulness pays off.

Recommended age: 11+

Robert Silverberg
The Book of Skulls
Gollancz

Four American college friends set out on a motoring expedition to discover a monastery hidden in the middle of the Arizona desert. They have read about it in an ancient document called *The Book of Skulls,* which claims that the monks there have discovered the secret of eternal life. But anyone wishing to share this knowledge must arrive at the monastery in a group of four. After that, it will be necessary for one of the group eventually to be killed and for another to commit suicide. The remaining two can then enter into immortality. After a number of quarrels, disagreements and reconciliations, this ill-matched modern quartet finally make it to their chosen destination. But which two will survive?

No short summary can do justice to this brilliant, disturbing and beautifully written novel, which keeps

into the future

readers in a state of tension from first page to last. Each character has a turn at telling the story while also unconsciously revealing themselves in all their various strengths and weaknesses. At the climax, each also has to confront the one, great personal secret they had always resolved to keep to themselves. Before that they sometimes behave like ordinary students and at other moments reach new levels of understanding. The monks, meanwhile, keep them under constant surveillance, locking them in at night while preparation for the final outcome goes remorselessly ahead. This haunting novel has all the qualities of a nightmare that is just too interesting ever to want to cut short.

Recommended age: 15+

Robert Swindells
Brother in the Land
Puffin

When Robert Swindells wrote *Brother in the Land* in the mid-1970s, it was one of many books that considered what might happen in the event of a nuclear war – a threat that seemed alarmingly near at the time. Its enduring strength lies in Robert Swindells' courage in telling the story for real, with no fairy-tale ending, although a new final chapter added in 2000 does offer a glimmer of hope.

This is our own world, now hideously distorted but still recognizable, and survivors have to make the best of it. Danny is out on the moors when the attack changes his life for ever. He is one of the lucky

into the future

survivors, but survival comes at a huge price – as Danny is soon to find out. Taking charge of his younger brother, he joins the other survivors as they meet new and unforeseen perils in this unfamiliar world. The urgent need for uncontaminated water and the desperation for anything safe to eat – these are the most important things in Danny's life. And he'll fight for them, breaking

all the rules if he must. But avoiding death from the blast turns out to have been a cruel irony, as radiation sickness begins to take its toll – and the long-term consequences look even more frightening.

Robert Swindells stresses the horrific realities that nuclear fallout would bring, but without sensationalism. The only redemption lies in the goodness of a few, including Kim, who becomes Danny's partner, making this a touching love story, despite its grim background.

Recommended age: 13+

Kurt Vonnegut
Slaughterhouse 5
Vintage

Billy Pilgrim's headlong travels through time include a

into the future

visit to Tralfamadore somewhere in space. Captured by the little green crewmen of a space ship, he is displayed naked in a zoo before being publicly mated with a voluptuous film star. But though in a different galaxy, Tralfamadore and the things that happen there are no odder than the places and times in our own galaxy, which Billy slips in and out of so easily. A wealthy optometrist by profession, Billy is an innocent in whatever world he finds himself, not least when he gets caught up in Germany at the end of World War II. Billy's account of his time there is both horrific and comical. Terrible acts of destruction and random moments of horror are let fall with no more comment than 'So it goes', a phrase that becomes a much-repeated refrain throughout the book.

Despite its fantastical structure, *Slaughterhouse 5* is essentially an anti-war novel written by Vonnegut in response to the events he had seen during World War II, in particular the RAF's bombing of Dresden. Sometimes employing comedy, sometimes tragedy, Vonnegut spins the reader through a furiously paced kaleidoscope of scenes and characters that capture both the chaos of war and its futility.

Recommended age: 15+

H.G. Wells
The Time Machine
Everyman

In the warmth of a dining room in a prosperous Victorian town house, the Time Traveller (who is never named) is entertaining some of his male friends. He tells them about the incredible journey he has recently made into the future on the Time Machine he has invented. Travelling to the year 802701, he discovered a world where humanity is divided into two groups. There are the handsome and childish Eloi, who spend much of their time doing little more than gathering flowers, singing and dancing. They live in luxury on the surface of the earth, but below, in dark, dank surroundings dwell the Morlocks. These hideous creatures work the machinery that keeps the upper world going. But to his horror, the Time Traveller discovers that they also use the helpless Eloi as a source of food. Quitting this evil place, the Time Traveller goes 30 million years further into the future to a time when the sun has cooled and life no longer exists. Returning home, he makes one more journey to prove to his disbelieving friends that he really is telling the truth. He is never seen again.

H.G. Wells was one of the most independent thinkers of his time. He published this short story in 1895, as a warning about what could eventually happen if the Western world continued to support a class structure where the rich few lived lives of luxury at the expense of the labouring poor. Unless there was a fairer way of doing things, Wells believed that one day the poor would take a terrible revenge upon their increasingly pampered oppressors. He also thought that if science was properly harnessed by society it would then be possible for everyone to lead easier lives, but only if there was a willingness to make political change.

into the future

This story has proved immensely popular with film makers. With his other fantasy novel, *The War of the Worlds* (1898), Wells established himself as one of the first science fiction writers.

Recommended age: 13+

into the future

real lives

Maya Angelou
I Know Why The Caged Bird Sings
Virago

I Know Why The Caged Bird Sings charts a life of extraordinary physical and emotional resilience with great passion (and no bitterness), never diminishing the author's suffering but not wallowing in it either. Most of Maya Angelou's childhood was spent with her grandmother, who was a formidable influence. Growing up in poverty in Arkansas in the

1930s, Angelou lived through racist times, with white people having unquestioned supremacy over blacks. It was never something that the young Maya could accept, and that rejection was formative to her development. But her life story is not just a statement about being black, it is also about a young girl growing up and finding her way in her own community, and eventually – after many pitfalls – making her own way in the world.

This is how Angelou describes the book: 'I write about being a Black American woman; however, I am always talking about what it's like to be a human being. This is how we are, what makes us laugh, and this is

real lives

how we fall and how we somehow, amazingly, stand up again.' It is this universal understanding and compassion, as well as the inspiring example of the author, that makes *I Know Why The Caged Bird Sings* so worth reading.

Recommended age: 13+

Livia Bitton-Jackson
I Have Lived for a Thousand Years
Simon & Schuster

'Only one who was there can truly tell the tale. And I was there.' So begins this memoir by Livia Bitton-Jackson, formerly Elli Friedman, who from May 31, 1944 managed to survive one of the worst Nazi concentration camps. From a normal life in Hungary, she and her family gradually lose their freedom as the new German invaders take over. Having left their home to live in a cramped ghetto, Elli and her mother finally end up at Auschwitz, where her mother falls ill. After smuggling her out of hospital, where she would certainly have died, Elli manages to escape in spite of being selected for the gas chambers. Instead, she joins her mother on a series of train journeys as the Allies gradually close in. She miraculously meets her brother again, and the three are liberated by American soldiers on April 30,1945. Learning of Elli's father's death, they decide to emigrate to America.

This is a story of triumph as well as tragedy. Nothing can ever soften the pain of the various humiliations Elli

real lives

had to survive, from having her head shaved, being whipped by the guards, offered only disgusting food and worked almost to death. She also witnesses things no one should have to see, let along a girl still aged only 13. Inmates are beaten, wounded and sometimes shot in front of her, and columns of children are led into the gas chambers in full view. But although there is nothing much Elli can do, she still keeps up her spirits in the most dreadful circumstances. Her story is both terrible and inspiring, however painful to read.

Recommended age: 13+

Bill Bryson
Notes From a Small Island
Black Swan

Bill Bryson travels the length and breadth of Great Britain, summing up the characteristics of the people and places he visits. It's the stories he tells about his responses to places, rather than any special facts he unearths, that make *Notes From a Small Island* so entertaining and often hugely funny.

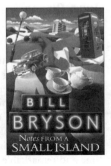

As an American who has lived in Britain for some time, he is generally a benevolent commentator, although never shy of saying exactly what he thinks. He can be bitingly critical of small-town mentalities, using telling anecdotes to make his points, and there are certain important things that he deplores – such as the destruction of Britain's heritage, as buildings and neighbourhoods are arbitrarily pulled down. But he also indulges some bitingly witty personal prejudices, such as his hatred of people in queues who don't get out their purses until they reach the checkout. There are useful warnings, too – such as not going on the Mersey ferry unless you can bear to have Gerry and the Pacemakers' song on the subject in your head for the next eleven days. But ultimately what makes *Notes From a Small Island* more than the sum of its jokes is Bill Bryson's ability to conjure up a place in a thumb-nail sketch and to bring it to life, all the way from sea-side resorts to ancient cathedral cities.

Recommended age: 15+

Jung Chang
Wild Swans
HarperCollins

Despite the horrors that Jung Chang reveals, *Wild Swans* is an uplifting story of individual courage and survival. Almost a century of complex and brutal Chinese history is covered through the life stories of three women – Jung Chang's grandmother, her mother and herself. The book provides a background to their personal tales, showing that they were both of their time and remarkable individuals in their own right.

real lives

The lives of the three women were completely different from each other, as China changed from the ancient repression of the emperors to the modern repression of the communists.

> **At the age of fifteen my grandmother became the concubine of a warlord general, the police chief of a tenuous national government of China. The year was 1924 and China was in chaos.**

Born at the beginning of the twentieth century, Jung Chang's grandmother was one of the last generation who suffered the lifelong agony of bound feet – a practice all too painfully described. At 15, she became first the concubine, then the wife, of a Chinese warlord. Women were entirely submissive and her life was spent in devotion to his every wish; it was only after his death and her remarriage that she had any measure of freedom. Life for De-hong, Jung Chang's mother, could hardly have been more different: she was still a child when Japan took control of China, imposing a harsh regime on the native population. She became an adult as the communists swept through the country, creating an entirely new social system in which she and her husband were to play active and senior parts.

Jung Chang herself was a child of the People's Revolution, brought up in a 'new' China but, sadly, one in which there was almost as much violence as there had been in her grandmother's day.

Recommended age: 15+

real lives

Roald Dahl
Going Solo
Puffin

The author's first volume of
autobiography, *Boy,* ends
when he is aged 20 and about
to sail away to East Africa.
This book continues the
story, starting with the
voyage where, as always, Dahl
manages to meet a succession
of weird characters all, as he
puts it, 'as potty as a
pilchard'. Once in Dar es
Salaam, which he loves, Dahl
has various adventures

involving wild animals, including one when a lion runs
away with the cook's wife clamped in his jaws. But any
sense of life as a permanent exotic picnic ends when
war is declared and Dahl joins the RAF to help defend
the Suez Canal. Despite a terrible crash where he
suffers badly from burns and broken bones, he
eventually makes it back into flying and this time is
sent to support the British troops left in Greece. Facing
certain defeat, he does as best he can before being one
of the last to leave.

Dahl is one of those authors incapable of writing a
dull sentence. So when he is describing the highly
dramatic events of his youth, the result is a feast of a
book, further enlivened with photos and extracts from

his diaries and letters at the time. It is difficult to think of any more readable chunk of autobiography than this one. Since much of it is taken up with war, readers can expect some sadness among all the jokes and adventures, and such is certainly the case in this book. But one reason Dahl has always been popular is that he never talks down to an audience. Instead, here is someone with a good story to tell and plenty of time to tell it.

Recommended age: 11+

Michael J. Fox
Lucky Man
Ebury Press

When Michael J. Fox wakes up one morning with trembling in his left hand, he knows something odd is happening. It could just be the result of too many late nights and a head-ringing hangover – he is, after all, in the middle of shooting a movie somewhere in Florida, and these things easily happen when on location. But this is something different. It takes over a year of questions before Fox finds out exactly what had made his hand tremble so uncontrollably, leading to the answer that he has 'a progressive, degenerative and

real lives

incurable neurological disorder' – Parkinson's disease. A top-rank movie star with a busy filming schedule, Fox kept his diagnosis secret for seven years while he searched for treatment and tried to stave off the inevitable progression of his illness.

In *Lucky Man* he tells the story of his life: his childhood in Canada, where he took part in every school production possible before moving fast into TV and films; his career as a film actor including his starring role in *Back to the Future*; his love affair with Tracy and the birth of his children. And then how his attitude to all of that is changed when he learns the shocking news that he has the long, hard struggle of living with Parkinson's disease ahead of him. Michael J. Fox writes with gentle irony and no self-pity so that, despite the tragedy at its heart, it is a thrilling story of courage, survival and hope.

Recommended age: 15+

Anne Frank
The Diary of a Young Girl
Penguin

In July 1942 Anne Frank, her family and four others hid in the back of an Amsterdam warehouse. They were trying to avoid the German occupiers of Holland, who were rounding up all Jews in order to deport them to concentration camps. Anne was only 13 when she started out on her new life in the secret annexe. She stayed there for over two years before the whole group was betrayed in August 1944. Her diary ends at that point; Anne went on to die of typhus at Auschwitz, just two months before it was liberated by British troops in April 1945.

> 66 I hope I will be able to confide everything to you, as I have never been able to confide in anyone, and I hope you will be a great source of comfort and support. 99

Only Anne's father survived of the original eight, and it was he who published her diary after the war. At the time he made a few cuts of material he thought too private for general circulation. But after his death in 1980 the full text of the diary finally appeared, which is the version recommended here. Included are some references by Anne to her own developing sexuality, plus a few catty remarks about her mother and the other residents. These are entirely in keeping with Anne's lively spirit and sparkling wit, where everything that happens is made interesting, especially when it is a matter of her own body changing in front of her. This diary remains one of the most moving documents to emerge from World War II, written by a person whose early death was a terrible as well as a pointless crime.

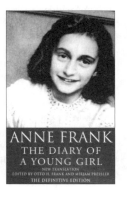

ANNE FRANK
THE DIARY OF
A YOUNG GIRL
NEW TRANSLATION
EDITED BY OTTO H. FRANK AND MIRJAM PRESSLER
THE DEFINITIVE EDITION

Recommended age: 11+

real lives

Nick Hornby
Fever Pitch
Penguin

To describe the author of
this book as a football fan
would be a massive under-
statement. He doesn't just
like football; he adores it,
devours it, thinks constantly
about it and – above all –
worries about it. As a lifetime Arsenal fan, he is in
agonies every time his team
plays, and even if they win
there is then the next game
to get nervous about. He
knows very well that football

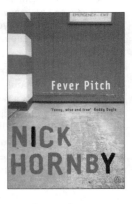

is just a game, of course, but is powerless to do
anything about his obsession. However badly some
individual players may perform, however cold and wet
it may be on the terraces, however irritable others may
become when his thoughts perpetually stray back to the
football pitch – Hornby has to carry on in the way he
always has.

> **❝** I fell in love with football as I was later
> to fall in love with women: suddenly, inexplica-
> bly, uncritically, giving no thought to the pain
> or disruption it would bring with it. **❞**

real lives

This book is the story of how this love affair started. Written with penetrating insight, it is about far more than just one person's obsession. Hornby also takes on the whole business of growing up from boy to man, the odd nature of families, issues of social class and the very nature of what passes for masculinity in modern Britain. This may sound heavy going, but his study is so delightfully written and contains so many excellent jokes that it has won over readers of both sexes and all ages, regardless of whether they actually enjoy football or not. Other immensely popular books by Hornby which, like this one, were also made into successful films include *High Fidelity* and *About a Boy*. But *Fever Pitch* is still his masterpiece, and without doubt the finest, most wide-ranging and often hilarious study of football and its supporters ever written.

Recommended age: 13+

Frank McCourt
Angela's Ashes
Flamingo

Without any power to change the course of his own history, the young Frank McCourt observes the terrible hardships of his childhood. He was born in Brooklyn, New York to young Irish Catholics, who flee unhappy memories and the impossible poverty of the Great Depression and take 4-year-old Frank back to Limerick, the home of his mother's family. Here the rapidly growing family lives in even greater poverty in a

real lives

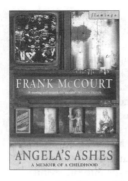

country dominated by never-ending rain. Frank's father is an optimistic alcoholic, quite unable to provide for his family; his mother, worn out by endless pregnancies and grief-stricken by the premature death of Frank's baby sister and twin brothers, maintains a deep faith in the Catholic Church. Along with his brothers and sisters, Frank struggles barefoot and hungry to school, stealing when necessary just to keep alive, until he has to leave and earn a living. Finally, like his parents, he emigrates to the US in search of a better life.

> **When I look back on my childhood I wonder how I survived at all. It was, of course, a miserable childhood: the happy childhood is hardly worth your while.**

The stark facts of Frank McCourt's life make grim reading and the number of child deaths, including the first girl Frank loves, make it impossible to ignore the ravages of poverty. But *Angela's Ashes* is also full of gallows humour – such as in the glorious scene when the landlord calls, only to find that the McCourt family has burnt all the walls in a desperate attempt to keep warm.

Recommended age: 15+

real lives

Jessica Mitford
Hons and Rebels
Orion

This memoir starts with the author and her sisters
being hunted by bloodhounds through the family
estate. But it is not in any way a horror story, since the
girls and the dogs were in fact devoted to each other
and this was a favourite game for both parties. Jessica
lived with her large family in Oxfordshire, the daughter
of a titled Lord who had read only one book in his life.
But her childhood took in many more eccentricities
than this. Absented from school in case they developed
bad habits, the girls spent most of the day living in
their own imaginative world, only occasionally
interrupted by a few lessons picked up from whoever
happened to be around to teach them. Demanding a
more organized education when such aimless boredom
finally became too much for her, Jessica went on to
become the family rebel in other ways, too, and married
the left-wing son of another noble family. The story
ends in the 1930s, when she hears of her husband's
death in the Spanish Civil War.

Possessed of a savage wit, Jessica is continually
amusing on the subject of her parents, their friends and
her own five sisters and one brother. Most of them
seem to have been odd in a number of ways which she
describes with relish. She also gives an unforgettable
picture of life in the aristocracy as it once was, with the
big country house and its servants carrying on as usual
however great the social changes happening outside. In

real lives

reaction to all this, Jessica eventually became a communist, playing a courageous part in the American civil rights movement during the 1960s. But she always saw the comic side of her strange childhood, as did her sister Nancy, who wrote about it in her bestselling novel *In Pursuit of Love*. Seldom can any family have contained two such witty sisters.

Recommended age: 13+

Michael Palin
Pole to Pole
BBC Books

Having famously travelled around the world in eighty days, Michael Palin found himself being driven insane by the number of different eighty-day exploits people suggested that he might try to make. So he decided to do a different one. He began a new journey, from one Pole to

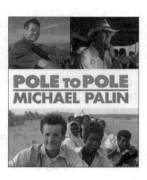

another following the 30-degree-east line of longitude. The trip took most of five months to complete and took Palin and his team through seventeen countries, with over seventy overnight stops. Avoiding aeroplanes as far as possible, they travelled on trains, trucks, rafts, buses, bicycles, balloons – and anything else that would take them the next step on their epic journey.

Palin's interest in the places he visits is infectious. He is curious about people and how they live their lives, and is good at capturing the essence of particular cultures. He is readily amused – by individuals, the strange antics of animals, the vagaries of different kinds of transport, but his laugher is always kind, never jeering. He never patronizes either the people he is describing or the audience he is writing for. Above all, he is healthily aware of the underlying quaintness of the whole caper, revelling in his mishaps with a pleasing sense of 'I know I'm mad'.

Recommended age: 13+

David Pelzer
A Child Called It
Orion

David Pelzer's account of his childhood chills to the core. The cruelty of his mother is almost unbelievable, and his detailing of it is seriously disturbing, as she finds one kind of torture after another to inflict on him. The failure of his father to protect him is also inexplicable and profoundly uncomfortable. And yet there is something about the young David's resilience in the face of such horror that makes *A Child Called It* transcend the simple boundaries of shock, and which makes it strangely heart-warming too.

On the surface, David's mother was a normal, caring mother. She loved her children – all except for David.

real lives

Not that she ever called him that; she only ever called him 'It'. Throughout his childhood, he was treated differently from his siblings. His mother inflicted a series of the most unimaginable and savage physical and mental tortures on him. Occasionally she claimed there was a reason behind what she did, but mostly the beatings, the burnings and the starving were unprovoked; unhinged by alcoholism, she let out her aggression on David. He survived by refusing to be crushed, perhaps recognizing even as a child that the cause lay within his mother rather than within himself. He tells the story of his life with a curious innocence, which makes him seem as much like a detached observer of these horrors as the person to whom they occurred.

Recommended age: 15+

Joe Simpson
Touching the Void
Vintage

One of the most unlikely stories of survival ever written, *Touching the Void* is even more remarkable because it's true. Joe Simpson wrote the book to make sure that the story of his miraculous survival was properly told. Top mountaineers Joe and his friend Simon Yates were climbing in the Peruvian Andes. They were almost at the summit, over 20,000 feet up, when Joe fell and smashed into the cliff below, breaking his leg. His chances of getting off the mountain alive seemed almost non-existent, but, roped to Simon and helped every inch by him, they slowly made their way down in a feat of unimaginable endurance. So far so good, but then fresh disaster struck. Still roped to Simon, Joe fell over an edge and was stranded, hanging in space. Simon couldn't get down to Joe and Joe couldn't get back up to Simon. Worse still, Joe's weight was gradually pulling Simon over

the edge too. Desperate, Simon had to take a terrible decision. He cut the rope, knowing that he was sending Joe to his death. But Joe didn't die; he was inching his way back to safety, whereas Simon had to try and come to terms with what he had done and face criticism from outside the climbing community.

> ❝ I saw the rope flick down, and my hopes sank. I drew the slack rope to me, and stared at the frayed end. Cut! I couldn't take my eyes from it. White and pink nylon filaments sprayed out from the end. ❞

Joe Simpson's story is unparalleled as an account of the sheer physical determination of climbers, while the moral dilemma of Simon's choice brings an unusual insight into the emotional links between extreme risk-takers.

Recommended age: 15+

real lives

graphic novels

Raymond Briggs
When the Wind Blows
Penguin

Hilda and Jim Bloggs are just an ordinary retired couple trying to do their best. Jim keeps himself up to date with the world by reading in the library; he knows that the international situation is bad, but he's sure that if he and Hilda follow the rules everything will be all right – just as it was in World War II, which they both survived. Jim carefully reads the official leaflets he's collected from the library and tries to make sense of them, while Hilda worries about keeping up standards. They seal up the windows, make a shelter in the house, gather in food supplies for fourteen days – including ordering 28 pints of milk – and collect the paper bags they are to climb into for safety (though Jim thinks that may be a joke). And then the bomb drops.

When the Wind Blows is written as a strip cartoon interspersed with sinister full-page pictures as the bomb approaches and is dropped. Through the combination of illustrations and speech bubbles, it makes its points accessible to all. Raymond Briggs produced it in 1982, when the threat of nuclear war

was horribly real – so much so that the government was distributing information about how to survive in the event of an attack, information that was hopelessly inaccurate and inadequate. There could be no survival. A lifelong pacifist, Raymond Briggs sets out to show the utter helplessness of ordinary people caught up in government policy and propaganda they can't begin to understand.

Recommended age: 13+

René Goscinny and Albert Uderzo
The Asterix Series
Orion

Set in 50 BC, this famous strip-cartoon series features heroic Ancient Gauls living in a tiny corner of Brittany while engaged in a continuing struggle against their would-be occupiers, the Roman army of Julius Caesar. Running to 31 titles to date, the stories centre around the small but energetic figure of Asterix himself, backed up as always by his faithful band of friends. The secret of their success in war is a magic potion brewed by the resident druid priest, Getafix. Against them, the Romans have little chance, losing out in regular battles where no one is ever seriously hurt and humour still rules the day. But although there is much fun poked at this inefficient invading army, the Gauls don't escape either, coming over as self-important to a fault while noticeably lacking in any sense of self-criticism.

These adventures can be read on many levels. On the surface, they tell an exciting story of adventure, near-disaster and final rescue. But they are also wonderfully satirical, packed with visual jokes and prone to bringing in comically out-of-place modern innovations, such as advertising breaks in the gaps between events during a session at the Roman circus. They can also be seen as symbolic of France's own unwillingness to be swallowed up by alien cultural forces, principally the English language linked to American values that some in France see as a threat to the survival of their own traditions. Endlessly inventive and wittily illustrated, these books continue to set a new high in the strip-cartoon world, delighting audiences of all ages ever since the first title appeared in 1959.

Recommended age: 13+

Frank Miller
(with Klaus Janson and Lynn Varley)
Batman: The Dark Knight Returns
Titan Books

Batman and Robin were once the uncontested heroes of comic-strip art. But how might they look if they returned to modern times, where the idea of lone avengers settling matters on their own outside any legal framework seems far more problematic? This brilliant graphic novel explores such an idea, re-creating Robin as a girl in the process. Another female character, the new police chief of Gotham City where the action is set, takes a very dim view of Batman, seeing him as a 'social fascist' whom she is determined to arrest for his frequent breaches of the peace. But Batman himself

graphic novels

knows there is still a massive task to do, since his old enemy The Joker threatens again as society crumbles and a war of total extermination becomes ever more likely.

Told in a comic strip that constantly changes in size, colour and emphasis, this is a story that demands to be read many times. Sometimes confusing but always highly dramatic, it teems with ideas that deserve to be taken seriously however grimly entertaining. Written many years before terrorism became an urgent issue for America, it prophesied the type of urban disaster that has since sadly become a reality, right down to details such as planes deliberately crashing into buildings. Often violent, sometimes disturbing but always thoughtful, this extraordinary book ends with an unforgettable climax as Batman and Superman engage in a final fight with the whole future of the world at stake.

Recommended age: 13+

Alan Moore and Dave Gibbons
Watchmen
Titan Books

This superb book, first published in 1986 but still as mesmerising as ever, set new standards for the graphic novel. Its tells the story of a small group of masked avengers, also known as minutemen or extra-normal operatives, who have been laid off with nothing more to do. Their urban American world meanwhile is visibly disintegrating as street crime soars under the growing threat of World War III. So it is no surprise when they are all finally persuaded by the thoroughly daunting Rorschach to make one more effort to save humanity. Although known to be 'crazier than a snake's armpit', Rorschach finally emerges as the main hero of this story where the real threat to the future turns out to come from one of these 'masks' themselves. His aim is to get rid of all the others, so leaving him free to engineer a nuclear explosion with the ultimate aim of forcing every country to work closer together in the future.

No verbal summary can adequately describe this amazing tale and the comic-strip illustrations with which it is so brilliantly told. Perspective constantly changes, sometimes swooping in for a close-up, at other times moving away into long shot. The pictures themselves tell the story not only as it unfolds but also, by using flashbacks, relating what had happened to the various characters in the past. At other moments illustrations show the different fantasies going on in the characters' minds as

graphic novels

they try to deal with their own troubled personalities as well as with all the problems of the world outside. Pessimistic, blackly amusing and fiercely intelligent, *Watchmen* offers a reading experience like no other and should not be missed.

Recommended age: 15+

Joe Sacco
Palestine
Jonathan Cape

The harsh face of occupied Palestine is made unforgettable by Joe Sacco in his nine comic-book stories which record the winter he spent living in the West Bank and Gaza Strip in 1991–92. Taken from conversations and observations and published for the first time in a single volume, this is the story of how the people of Palestine live with the violence which affects their daily lives. Much of the detail is brutal and shocking which makes the overall impact disturbing and uncomfortable but Sacco is never gratuitous in his use of horror. Told through the eyes of a bumbling, harmless-looking Western journalist, Sacco records without judgement the stories of Sameh, Ammar, Ghassan and others – men whose lives have been derailed by false arrests, interrogation, lack of work and extreme poverty. Words and pictures are equally powerful in revealing the desperate plight of Palestine as its economy is crushed and its social fabric destroyed. But these stories are full of human warmth, too. The importance of family, friendship and loyalty underpins everyone's lives, giving reasons for survival and cooperation in the face of such danger.

Sacco varies the way the different stories are told – some are mostly pictures with speech bubbles, others rely on longer narratives – but however he does it, *Palestine* provides a startling insight into the long-running Israeli-Palestinian conflict.

Recommended age: 13+

Posy Simmonds
Gemma Bovery
Jonathan Cape

Love of all kinds – and its complications – is brilliantly explored in Posy Simmonds' *Gemma Bovery*, a loose take on Flaubert's classic novel *Madame Bovary*. Simmonds is penetratingly acute on everything she sees, and the bonus of the graphic form is that several stories can be told at the same time – especially appropriate here, where Gemma's many complex affairs can be unravelled simultaneously.

graphic novels

Raymond Joubert, an ageing poet turned baker, tells the story of Gemma, a young English girl who arrives in France with her partner Charlie in search of a better life. Joubert is immediately smitten by her and views the couple longingly. Initially ecstatic about France and all things French, especially the food, Gemma soon becomes bored and dissatisfied with the primitiveness of country life and finds a young lover while always, always dreaming of her former lover in England – the upper-class Patrick, who has oodles of slimy charm. Joubert follows Gemma around, making up stories about her and torturing himself as she pursues her passions.

Posy Simmonds' commentary on the foibles of everyone is hilarious. She has an unerring ability to pick out weakness, whether she's portraying a place or a person – especially when it's details of snobbishness or counter-snobbishness, or the differences between the French and the English – in a way that's wickedly barbed but never malicious.

Recommended age: 15+

graphic novels

Art Spiegelman
The Complete Maus
Penguin

This moving and unforgettable story is a documentary and memoir as well as a comic book. It is based on the true story of the author-illustrator's father, a Jew who somehow managed to survive life in a wartime concentration camp. In 1945 he made it to America in order to start again. But the memories of this cantankerous old man refuse to go away, and are told here in comic-book form. Rather than go in for total realism, Spiegelman provides some distance from the sheer horror of this account by portraying all the Nazis as cats, the Jews as mice and the Poles, in whose country these grim adventures took place, as dogs. In between recalling the events of the past, father and son continue their often troubled relationship into the present, quarrelling at one moment, forgiving each other the next.

There are also many genuinely comic moments, particularly when that Spiegelman records the various things his parents do that always manage to irritate him. But he is constantly drawn back to them, particularly to his father and the terrible tales he has to tell about a past that never fades. Readers are left with a feeling of sadness and wonder that people could possibly be so needlessly cruel towards each other. Yet this is also a story of survival on the part of someone determined to get by, come what may. Brilliantly illustrated and told as if the old man were speaking out

graphic novels

aloud, this extraordinary book is never anything less than totally involving.

Recommended age: 13+

Chris Ware

Jimmy Corrigan: The Smartest Kid on Earth

Jonathan Cape

The pathos of Jimmy Corrigan's life – growing up without his real father while constantly inventing the kind of father he would have liked to have – is brilliantly captured in Chris Ware's emotionally telling strip cartoons. Looking small and insignificant on the page, Jimmy is a 'nobody' who longs to get away from his mother and forge relationships with the girls in his office. He tries hard to create a father figure whom he can both love and respect; a Superman hero is his ideal but other, less impressive fathers would do as well. Anybody but the violent man he remembers so vividly.

Jimmy's world is full of fears and setbacks and his responses are timorous and apparently ineffective. But gradually he makes some headway in his life including,

graphic novels

finally, making a date with the new girl in the office. Although they seem specific, Jimmy's fears embrace universal anxieties about identity and self-worth and his frailties always evoke sympathy. As so often with strip cartoons, the apparent simplicity of the pictures disguises the huge range of complex emotions on display. Equally enjoyable whether it's dipped into or read as a continuous narrative, *Jimmy Corrigan* is a moving story of a man struggling to find an identity, and told in a manner in which words and pictures perfectly complement each other.

Recommended age: 15+

graphic novels

Meg Cabot
The Princess Diaries
Macmillan

With her life revolving around shopping, friends and hanging out, Mia's just an ordinary teenager. At least that's what she thinks – until her father suddenly announces that she's a princess. No longer Mia Thermopolis, Mia is now Amelia Mignonette Grimaldi Thermopolis Renaldo, Princess of Genovia. Mia isn't much like a princess and she has no plans to become girly or posh, but will she be able to cope with the pressure? And will being a princess make all the daily problems of life any easier?

Mia tells the story of her adjustment in a sharply observed diary of teenage life that pours out in a chatty, confiding flow. She records all the important – and trivial – things that happen to her. There's her mother's burgeoning relationship with the algebra teacher (fairly gross, especially when you think of them kissing). There's her father, with his string of pretty but impossibly young girlfriends whom he dumps after only a week or two. And then there's her difficult Grandmère, who only approves of certain friends. Above all, there's the question of Mia's own

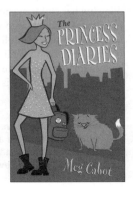

humour

friends – and particularly her success (and failure) with different boys.

Recommended age: 11+

Gerald Durrell
My Family and Other Animals
Penguin

Gerald Durrell's gift for straight-telling the outrageous stories from his childhood makes *My Family and Other Animals* very funny indeed. To escape the grey English weather, the unconventional Durrell family take off for Corfu. Gerry, as he is universally known, arrives in Corfu with 'a butterfly net, a dog and a jam-jar full of caterpillars all in imminent danger of turning into chrysalids'. Corfu is the perfect place for him to pursue his naturalist's enthusiasm – as well as to observe the foibles of his family. His mother is deliciously vague, allowing her children enormous freedom to go about their own affairs: Margo sunbathes in a skimpy swim-suit, thus attracting a following of local lads despite her obvious disdain; Leslie indulges in his passion for shooting (with some hair-raising and unexpected results); Larry sets up his two trunks of books and settles down to write.

> 66 This must have been the first tortoise of spring, and as if his appearance from the subterreanean dormitory was a signal, the hills suddenly became covered with tortoises. 99

humour

Against this noisy background, the 10-year-old Gerry, always accompanied by his dog – and often with a string of strays following behind – explores the beautiful island, treasuring animals and insects of all kinds. Each is named and befriended, quickly joining the already bizarre Durrell household. Among others, there's Madame Cyclops the turtle and Ulysses the owl, a magpie, some water snakes and a scorpion. Gerry loved them all and his observations about their lives are hilarious.

Recommended age: 13+

Anne Fine
Flour Babies
Puffin

Fourteen-year-old Simon Martin has never worked hard at school and has no intention of changing his ways. At all times amiable, he still remains popular with his teachers and his mother, even though they have given up hope of seeing any progress. But after an unexpected lesson in child development, Simon and his mates are each presented with a large bag of flour. The only rule is that they must always carry it around with them wherever they go. After a spell of

doing that, the hope is that this will teach them something about what looking after a real baby might be like in terms of cutting down on personal freedom. Although Simon enters into the project in a spirit of mockery, he soon becomes more thoughtful. Could this whole experience give him any idea why his own father left the family only six weeks after Simon was born?

Anne Fine is a master of dialogue, and the often hilarious exchanges between Simon, his mates and their long-suffering teachers sound exactly like the real thing. The flour baby experiment actually happened in certain schools, and there are many other ways, too, where this story stays close to recognizable reality. Simon himself ends up with a far better understanding of his own mother and even a little more sympathy for his absent father. How a small sack of flour helps him come to these conclusions is both convincing and moving enough to affect even Mr Cartright, 4C's harassed but basically good-humoured science teacher. Anne Fine is always a brilliant writer, and particularly so in this marvellous story that comes over as both light-hearted and profound at the same time.

Recommended age: 11+

humour

Morris Gleitzman
Bumface
Puffin

Angus has a problem. While he would much rather be 'Bumface', the famous pirate of his imagination, he is in fact the sort of boy his mother can justifiably call 'Mr

Dependable'. Which is just as well, because Angus's mum, a soap opera star, just can't stop having a new baby every time she finds a new man. And who buys the food, cooks, changes the nappies and puts these babies to bed once they start growing up? Why, Mr Dependable, of course, even though it means he can never see his friends after school and could well lose his prized

place in the school play. To make matters worse, Angus's mum has just acquired a fourth man. Desperate to stop her having yet another baby, Angus swings into action as best he can with the help of his new Indian girlfriend Rindi. She, meanwhile, has her own problems, with a father trying to push her into a forced marriage.

Morris Gleitzman is a very funny writer, and just the opening sentence of this terrific story is enough to keep readers laughing for hours afterwards. But behind the humour he also has something important to say, in this case about the difficulties sometimes visited on young people by parents who aren't around when there is any domestic work to be done. Since Angus is a decent kid, he can't stand by and see his junior brother and sister neglected. But what about his own needs? So when he is told to grow up after deliberately wrecking his mother's publicity launch, he has the perfect answer:

humour

'Not yet.' Whether this will be enough to make his monstrously selfish parents think again is debatable, but at least Angus has made a point, not just for himself but for every other young person in anything like the same predicament.

Recommended age: 11+

George and Weedon Grossmith
The Diary of a Nobody
Penguin

City clerk Mr Pooter is no hero, but he is a decent if pompous man. His diary shows over and over again how the laugh is always on himself, however little he realises it. Given to cracking unfunny jokes, he regularly misses the point of much funnier ones. The best efforts of this socially ambitious man never quite come off. A visit to the theatre on complimentary tickets turns into a disaster. On another occasion, a ball at London's Mansion House goes horribly wrong after Pooter unwisely takes a second glass of champagne. But with the attentions of his two friends Gowing and Cummings, Mr Pooter is on the whole a contented man – if only his son Lupin could settle down to a similarly respectable life. There is, after all, always his diary to complain to on those many occasions when he feels life hasn't quite dealt him the hand he both wants and deserves.

This book has never been out of print since it first appeared in 1892. It was the first of many gentle satires, the humour of which is derived from the way that the

humour

main characters keep giving themselves away. Although Pooter comes over as a snob, narrow-minded and conceited, readers are never told this outright – it is simply evident in everything he writes. But he is also loyal to his friends and employers and forever romantic about his frequently irritable wife Carrie. So while readers can enjoy the gentle fun poked at him, there is never any feeling of distaste for Pooter himself. Minor characters come and go as the days pass, each with their own point of interest and occasional irritation for one of the truly great comic creations of all time.

Recommended age: 11+

Carl Hiaasen
Hoot
Macmillan

Roy has just moved to Florida, which he dislikes because it is so over-developed, with Disney World in his opinion little more than a giant armpit. There is also the problem posed by Dana Matherson, a vicious and uncouth school bully. But one day Roy sees a barefoot boy running for his life. Intrigued, he discovers that this boy, whose name remains a secret, is on a

humour

mission to save some rare burrowing owls whose nesting place is threatened by the arrival of a Pancake restaurant. Roy joins in this fight, making life hell for Curly, the grumpy and bald site foreman. But more formidable opposition comes from Chuck E. Muckle, the ruthless head of the whole Pancake chain. There is also still the threat of Dana, regularly outwitted by Roy but always dangerous.

The author has already written nine eco-thrillers for an adult market, always featuring lone protesters up against the might of American corporations out to enrich themselves no matter what the costs to the environment. This first novel for a younger audience should prove equally popular with all ages. It is stuffed with one-liners, ingeniously plotted and constantly exciting; reading can hardly ever come more pleasurable than this. And behind all the jokes and absurdities, Hiaasen has a serious point to make about the need to protect the surviving wildlife in the US. By communicating this message through humour, he remains one of the most readable of environmentally conscious writers as well as the funniest.

Recommended age: 11+

Hilary McKay
Saffy's Angel
Hodder

Saffy, short for Saffron, is one of an eccentric artistic family where all the children are named after different colours. Shortly into the story she discovers that she has

been adopted, and becomes determined to find out more about her past. In particular, she has a vivid memory of a stone angel when she was staying in Italy as a baby. Now teamed up with Sarah, a friend even more determined than herself, Saffy smuggles herself out to Siena. There, she and Sarah are in for some surprises before a happy ending. At home meanwhile, Saffy's older sister a love affair with her driving instructor while her mother carries on with painting pictures in the garden shed where she goes to escape all the various distractions caused by her unruly but fundamentally loving children.

There is more than a touch of *Cider With Rosie* in this description of a close-knit family which, however odd it may look to outsiders, continues to function pretty well within itself. Such fictional families can sometimes seem maddeningly complacent, but there is no touch of self-congratulation in these pages. The fact that Sarah is confined to a wheelchair is also treated not as a problem but simply as part of her own feisty character. Dipping into this novel is like overhearing a fascinating conversation conducted by others whom it would be very nice to know as friends. Written largely

humour

in dialogue, this engaging and affectionate story is bound to leave readers smiling. The same author also wrote *The Exiles,* another story about a comically wayward family so successful that it led to three more titles about the same charmingly chaotic characters.

Recommended age: 13+

Louise Rennison
Angus, Thongs and Full-Frontal Snogging
Scholastic

Fourteen-year-old Georgia Nicolson lives with her parents, little sister Libby and Angus the cat. She has a number of ridiculous relatives, all of whom still talk to her as if she is 5, is taught by a bunch of sadistic teachers in a school where not wearing a beret is a serious crime and, most important of all, is waiting for the Sex God – or even just an ordinary boyfriend – to turn up.

All this, and more, Georgia records in her diary: sometimes minute by minute; sometimes (especially when she's too busy with Robbie, the Sex God) with long gaps between entries. Whatever happens to Georgia, from the tragedy of not being allowed to sit in

the back row with her best friend to the nirvana of
being kissed by Robbie, her diary is outrageously funny,
even when it narrates what she sees as the mind-aching
boredom of just *being*. The intimate secrets of Georgia's
life are spot-on in tone, both realistic enough to be
convincing and embellished enough to be hilarious.

Recommended age: 11+

Rosie Rushton
Just Don't Make a Scene, Mum
Puffin

Five teenagers' lives are intertwined in this snappy
insight into how it feels to be growing up. Whatever
their particular difficulties, they all share one enormous
problem – parents.

Laura's parents are divorced and she's sure that the
whole world is conspiring against her. Her father has a
ghastly new girlfriend with two horrible children; and
her mum, instead of trying to do her best to get him
back, has taken up with the geeky Melvyn. No wonder
her own life is in ruins. Jemma's parents are hopelessly
out of date. Not only do they look ridiculous
themselves, but they want Jemma to look ridiculous
too. Her wardrobe houses a collection of clothes
suitable for a 9-year-old which, combined with her
parents calling her 'Petal' in public, makes it hard to
create the right impression. Jon's dad, meanwhile, wants
him to go to university and study law, especially after
having forked out for him to go to a posh school. But

humour

what do good grades matter compared to a night out at the Stomping Ground? Jon knows which he'll choose. Sumitha's parents have very clear views about what Bengali girls should and shouldn't do; meeting boys is definitely on the shouldn't list. Drama classes and ballet are fine, but the word 'disco' is forbidden. Chelsea's mum is no better. Despite being the agony aunt of the local radio station, apparently in tune with the young, she's the first to say no to staying out after 10.30, which doesn't exactly give Chelsea much scope. Rosie Rushton wittily charts the problems of being yourself when parents have ideas of their own.

Recommended age: 11+

James Thurber
A Thurber Carnival
Penguin

Heard about Walter Mitty, the mild-mannered husband who compensates for his wife's nagging by making up wonderful fantasies where he always plays the hero? Or Mr Bruhl, an ordinary enough citizen who starts to behave in a criminal manner simply because he looks like a notorious gangster in the news? Or the modern version of *Little Red Riding Hood,* which ends with the wolf shot dead by an automatic pistol? ('Moral: It is not so easy to fool little girls nowadays as it used to be.') Or *The Day the Dam Broke*, when everyone in a small town came to believe that a disaster had happened after one casual remark was first misheard and then fanned into a major panic?

These stories and many more came from the pen of James Thurber, an American humorist who was one of the funniest authors of his time (he died in 1961). He also drew brilliant cartoons, using very thick lines since his own eyesight was so poor (the subject of another of his inspired pieces, describing how he was always unable to see anything under the school microscope). Another favourite story is The *Topaz Cufflinks Mystery*, about a middle-aged man crouching by the roadside simply to prove to his wife in the family car stationed down the road that human eyes do not light up when caught by headlights. His wife, meanwhile, insists that they do; and many other equally pointless but hilarious husband-wife arguments find their way into these stories and cartoons.

Recommended age: 11+

Sue Townsend
The Queen and I
Arrow

Jack Barker, the leader of the newly elected People's Republican Party, has news for the Queen. She and her family must move out of their house. Her new home

humour

will be a pensioner's bungalow, the same entitlement as for anyone else of her age. Her new address will be 9 Hellebore Close (renamed Hell Close by its inhabitants), a housing estate somewhere in the Midlands. And the list of things she can take with her is a short one: there is to be only one dog per household, no horses – much to Charles's regret – and, as Diana points out, no clothes.

> ❝ The Queen was in bed watching television with Harris. It was election night, 11.20pm, Thursday 9 April 1992. Harris yawned, displaying his sharp teeth and liver-coloured tongue. ❞

This story of the how the Royals adapt to their strange, unfamiliar surroundings is hugely imaginative. Seen through the Queen's eyes, it captures the misery of poverty, the endless counting of pennies and worrying whether there's enough. Sue Townsend makes it hilarious but also pointed. And, while she laughs at the assumptions and attitudes of the Queen and her family, she is tender and kind about them as individuals. Caviar gives way to boiled eggs, and the Queen learns to make her own broth as she remembers her nanny Crawfie doing when she was ill as a little girl. The question is, will she be changed by being poor, or is she a queen whatever the circumstances?

Recommended age: 13+

Evelyn Waugh
Scoop
Penguin

William Boot, a gentle and innocent young bachelor, is perfectly happy living with his parents while writing a column about country life for a daily newspaper. But by a ridiculous mistake he is sent out to the remote and corrupt Ishmaelia – a fictitous African state – to cover a possible civil war. Completely out of his depth, William is so hopeless he is about to be sacked when he manages entirely by accident to dispatch the story every newspaper was hoping to get. Although the envy of all his fellow journalists and arousing the interest of the beautiful but heartless German girl Katchen, William still can't wait to return to the safety of the English countryside. And this time he makes sure there are no more mistakes, despite all the pressure to continue his career as a foreign correspondent.

Written in 1938, *Scoop* mocks everyone and everything in the world of journalism in a way that still

humour

makes sense today. It is also merciless in its satire of newly independent countries and the way that corruption can easily take over, despite all the fine words and promises. The tone of this book is in many ways appalling, with the author often coming over as both a racist and a snob. But as a true satirist he is pitiless about all human beings and institutions, and it would be a shame not to enjoy such acid humour and merciless wit. He also writes beautifully, never using two words where one would do and always hitting the nail on the head in page after page of biting, sometimes uncomfortable but always hilarious prose.

Recommended age: 15+

Geoffrey Willans and Ronald Searle
Molesworth
Penguin

Nigel Molesworth, 'the curse of St Custard's', is a far-from-ideal student. He first appeared as a cartoon character in *Punch* magazine before having a book all to himself in *Down With Skool!*, the first title in this anthology. He is irreverent, anarchic and irrepressible as he makes his way through education, jotting down his thoughts on teachers, rules and the

peculiarities of Latin. His main aim in life is to do as little work as possible and to get away with it, and this philosophy is perfectly expressed in his idiosyncratic spelling and equally quirky vocabulary – both of which never improve. In *How to be Topp!*, the second title, he offers advice on how to survive as a new kid, how to 'akquire culture' and 'Keep the Brane Clean', how to be a 'wizz' for games varying from 'criket' to 'conkers', how to cope with 'bulies', 'snekes' and grown-ups and, above all, how to be 'Topp in English'.

66 This is me e.g. nigel molesworth the curse of st custard's which is the skool i am at. It is utterly wet and weedy as i shall (i hope) make clear but of course that is the same with all skools. 99

Molesworth's cynical approach to school is the stuff of teachers' nightmares, but it is guaranteed to make him the most popular boy. Ronald Searle's brilliant illustrations of life at St Custard's are an integral part of Molesworth's long-lasting (and hopefully long-to-continue) career as one of the greatest and most memorable schoolboys in literature.

Recommended age: 11+

P.G. Wodehouse
Jeeves and Wooster Omnibus
Penguin

'What ho! Pip pip! Oh, I say! Right-o!' This can only be

humour

Bertie Wooster, the young bachelor of no great brains whose independent means ensure him a very pleasant, undemanding life. Unfortunately, along with his friends Gussie Fink-Nottle, Bingo Little and Tuppy Glossop, Bertie is apt to go in for hair-brained schemes whose success depends on temporary theft, deception or disguise. He is invariably caught out in the most compromising of situations, but relief unfailingly arrives in the shape of his butler Jeeves, he of the grave but sympathetic face. There is a cost, though. Should Bertie have purchased a tie Jeeves does not care for, or imprudently decided to grow a moustache that does not suit him, his butler will always see to it that his grateful employer finally sees the error of his ways.

Containing some of the finest comic writing in English, these stories are set in an idealised vision of Britain in which the idle rich seem to do little else but while away their time at clubs or attend an endless round of country house parties. Feckless young men keep falling for beautiful young women, not always for the best, in which case Bertie and Jeeves are usually on hand to help them escape. Bertie himself frequently makes rash promises to women with an alarming desire to reform his idle ways – something he has no interest in doing at all. Bertie must also contend with the disapproval and regular criticism of his formidable aunts – the bossy Dahlia and the fearsome Agatha.

The adventures of Jeeves and Wooster are told in several novels and collections of short stories, most of which are published by Penguin. A good place to start is the *Jeeves and Wooster Omnibus* which contains three of the best – *The Mating Season, The Code of the Woosters* and *Right Ho, Jeeves.*

Recommended age: 11+

humour

Index

Index

Index

Index

Index

TRAVEL • MUSIC • REFERENCE • PHRASEBOOKS

key: map   phrasebook   cd

Rough Guides publishes new books every

Las Vegas
Los Angeles ☻
Maui
Miami & the Florida
  Keys ☻
Montréal
New England
New Orleans
New York City ☻
New York City
  Mini Guide
New York
  Restaurants
Pacific Northwest
Rocky Mountains
San Francisco ☻
San Francisco
  Restaurants
Seattle
Skiing and
  Snowboarding in
  North America
Southwest USA
Toronto
USA
Vancouver
Washington DC ☻
Yosemite

**Caribbean
& Latin
America**
Antigua & Barbuda
Argentina ☻ ⊙
Bahamas
Barbados
Belize
Bolivia

Brazil
Caribbean
Central America
Chile
Costa Rica
Cuba ☻ ⊙
Dominican
  Republic ☻
Ecuador
First-Time Latin
  America
Guatemala ☻
Jamaica ☻
Maya World
Mexico ▣ ☻ ⊙
Peru ⊙
St Lucia
Trinidad &
  Tobago ☻

**Africa & Middle
East**
Cape Town
Egypt ▣ ☻ ⊙
Gambia ⊙
Israel & Palestinian
  Territories
Jerusalem
Jordan
Kenya ▣ ⊙
Morocco ☻
South Africa,
  Lesotho
  & Swaziland
  ▣ ☻
Syria
Tanzania ⊙
Tunisia
West Africa ⊙

Zanzibar
Zimbabwe ⊙

**Reference
Music**
Acoustic Guitar
Classical Music
Country Music
Country: 100
  Essential CDs
Cuban Music
Drum'n'bass
Flute
House
Irish Music
Jazz
Latin: 100 Essential
  CDs
Music USA
Opera
Reggae
Rock
Rock: 100 Essential
  CDs
Soul: 100 Essential
  CDs
Techno
World Music Vol1
World Music Vol2

Reference
The Beatles
Books for Teenagers
Children's Books,
  0–5
Children's Books,
  5–11
Cult Football

Cult Movies
Cult Pop
Cult TV
Digital Stuff
Elvis
Formula 1
History of China
History of Egypt
History of England
History of France
History of India
History of Islam
History of Italy
History of Spain
History of USA
The Internet
Internet Radio
James Bond
Man Utd
Personal Computers
Pregnancy & Birth
Shopping Online
Travel Health
Travel Online
Unexplained
  Phenomena
The Universe
Videogaming
Weather
Website Directory
Women Travel

Rough Guides music & reference

Informed, independent advice
on the major gaming platforms

Punchy reviews
of the top games in every genre

Hints, tips and cheats
to crack each game

Directories
of the best Web sites and gaming resources

The Rough Guide to Videogaming. £5.99